Sanborn Tenney

Pictures and stories of animals,

For the little ones at home

Sanborn Tenney

Pictures and stories of animals,
For the little ones at home

ISBN/EAN: 9783337815097

Printed in Europe, USA, Canada, Australia, Japan

Cover: Foto ©ninafisch / pixelio.de

More available books at **www.hansebooks.com**

PICTURES AND STORIES OF ANIMALS

FOR

THE LITTLE ONES AT HOME.

BY

Mrs. SANBORN TENNEY.

INSECTS, CRUSTACEANS, AND WORMS.
WITH ONE HUNDRED AND TWENTY-FOUR WOOD ENGRAVINGS.

NEW YORK:
SHELDON AND COMPANY,
498 AND 500 BROADWAY.
1868.

PREFACE.

BELIEVING that there is nothing in which children are naturally more interested than they are in animals, and that there are no other objects which can be used to greater advantage than these in their instruction, the writer has prepared these Pictures and Stories of Animals for the Little Ones, to instruct as well as to interest and amuse them.

There are six books in the series, each one complete in itself; and they are so arranged that together they make a Juvenile Library of the Natural History of Animals.

The first book contains pictures and stories of Mammals or Quadrupeds; the second book, pictures and stories of Birds; the third, of Reptiles and Fishes; the fourth, of Bees, Butterflies, and other

Insects, and of Crustaceans and Worms; the fifth, of Shells, and the animals which live in them; and the sixth, of Sea-Cucumbers, Sea-Urchins, Star-Fishes, Jelly-Fishes, Sea-Anemones, and Corals.

The wood engravings in the six books are more than five hundred in number, and are true to nature. Several of them were drawn and engraved expressly for this series; the others are mainly from Tenney's "Manual of Zoölogy," "Natural History of Animals," and other works of Tenney's Natural History Series.

August, 1868.

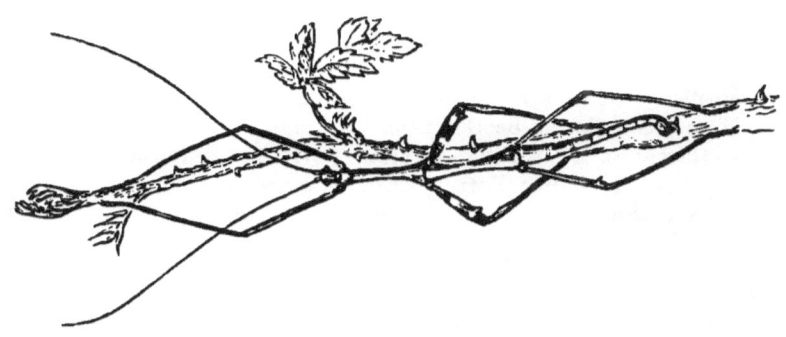

CONTENTS.

	PAGE
FIRST IDEAS ABOUT INSECTS	9–14

THE BEES, WASPS, &c., OR HYMENOPTERS.

The Honey-Bees — Humble-Bees — Carpenter-Bee — Tailor-Bee — Mason-Bee — Paper-making Wasps — Mud-Wasps — Ichneumons — Gall-Flies — Boring Saw-Fly — Saw-Flies 14–36

THE SCALY-WINGED INSECTS, OR LEPIDOPTERS.

The Asterias Butterfly — Turnus Butterfly — White Butterfly — Yellow Butterfly — Misippus Butterfly — Mountain Butterfly — Skippers — Moths — Five-spotted Sphinx — Humming-bird Moth, or Clear-winged Sesia — Peach-tree Borer — Beautiful Deiopeia — Salt-marsh, or Beach Moth — Silk-worm — American Silk-worm, or Polyphemus Moth — Luna Moth — Cecropia Moth — Promethea Moth — Tent-caterpillar Moth — Span-worms — Canker-worms — Leaf-rollers — Clothes Moths 37–70

THE TWO-WINGED INSECTS, OR DIPTERS.

The Mosquitoes — Wheat-Fly — Hessian-Fly — Crane-Flies — Black-Flies — House-Flies — Horse-Flies — Bot-Flies — Bee-Flies — Asilus-Flies 70–76

THE SHEATH-WINGED INSECTS, OR BEETLES, OR COLEOPTERS.

The Tiger-Beetles — Caterpillar-Hunter — Water Beetle — Carrion Beetle — Rove Beetle — Horn-Bug, or Stag

Beetle — Goldsmith Beetle — Dor-Bug — Phaneus — Buprestis — Spring-Beetles, or Snap-Beetles — Fire-Flies — Curculios, or Weevils — Painted Clytus — Beautiful Clytus — Apple-tree Borer — Broad-necked Prionus — Chrysomela — Cucumber Beetle — Lady-Bird . . 77–92

THE CICADAS, &c., OR HEMIPTERS.
 The Dog-day Cicada, or Harvest Fly — Seventeen-year Cicada — Tree-Hoppers — Plant-Lice — Scorpion-Bug — Squash-Bug 92–98

THE STRAIGHT-WINGED INSECTS, OR ORTHOPTERS.
 The Earwig — Cockroach — Walking-Stick — Mantis — Crickets — House-Cricket — White Climbing-Cricket — Mole Cricket — Katy-did — Grasshoppers — Locusts . 98–108

THE NERVE-WINGED INSECTS, OR NEUROPTERS.
 The May-Fly — Stone-Fly — Dragon-Fly — Horned Corydalis — Ant-Lion — Caddice-Fly 108–116

THE SPIDERS AND SCORPIONS 116–123

THE CENTIPEDES 124–126

THE CRABS, LOBSTERS, AND SHRIMPS 126–135

THE SAND-HOPPERS AND TRILOBITES 135–138

THE BARNACLES AND HORSE-SHOE CRAB . . . 138–142

THE WORMS 143–150

CONCLUDING WORDS 150

PICTURES AND STORIES OF ANIMALS.

DEAR CHILDREN:—

In this little book you will find pictures and stories of the Honey-Bee, of the Wasp and the curious nest it makes for its young ones, of the beautiful Butterflies which hover over the flowers in the daytime, and of the not less beautiful Moths which come out of their hiding-places and fly about at night, of Flies, Beetles, Cicadas, Grasshoppers, and Dragon-Flies, and of many other Insects; and of the Crabs, Lobsters, and Shrimps which live in the sea; and of the Worms, some kinds of which live in the sea and some upon the land.

The number of kinds of insects is very great, even hundreds of thousands.

Some kinds of insects have four thin wings, the hind pair being the smaller; two pairs of

A Bee, — an Hymenopter.

jaws, the upper pair for biting, and the lower for getting honey; and a sting or some other piercing organ. They are called the Hymenopters, or Membrane-winged Insects. Such are the Bees, Wasps, Ants, and Ichneumons.

Some kinds of insects have four wings, which

A Butterfly, — a Lepidopter.

are covered with minute scales that rub off when we touch them. These insects have a long tongue, which, when not in use, is coiled up beneath the head. They are called the Lepidopters, or Scaly-winged Insects. Such are the Butterflies and Moths.

Some kinds of insects, as Flies and Mosquitos, have only two wings; but in the place of hind

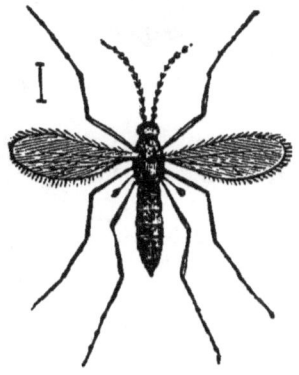

A Fly, — a Dipter.

wings they have two knobbed threads, or balancers, and they are called the Dipters, or Two-winged Insects.

Some kinds of insects have their forward or upper wings hard, and these wings meet in a straight line along the back, and they have the hind or under wings thin, and when they are not flying, these wings are folded and hidden

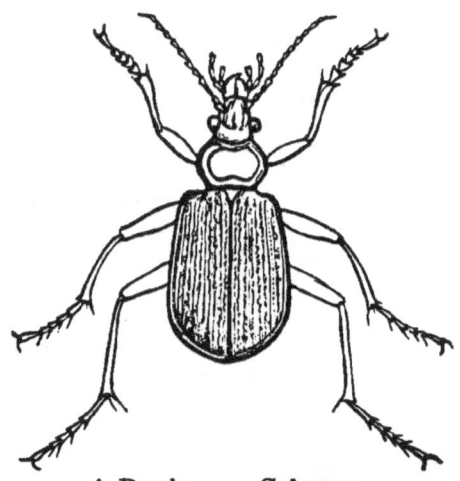

A Beetle, — a Coleopter.

beneath the hard and horn-like upper wings. Such Insects are called the Coleopters, or Beetles. They generally have a little triangular piece between the bases of the wings, as you see it in the picture.

Some kinds of insects, as the Cicadas, have a

A Cicada, — an Hemipter.

slender, horny beak, which, when not in use, is bent back under the body; and some kinds also have their wings thick near the body, and thin toward the end. These insects are called Hemipters.

A Grasshopper, — an Orthopter.

Some kinds of insects, as the Grasshoppers, have wings which lie straight along the top or sides of the back, and they are called the Straight-winged Insects, or Orthopters.

Some kinds of insects, as Dragon-Flies, have very large eyes, very large netted-veined wings, and

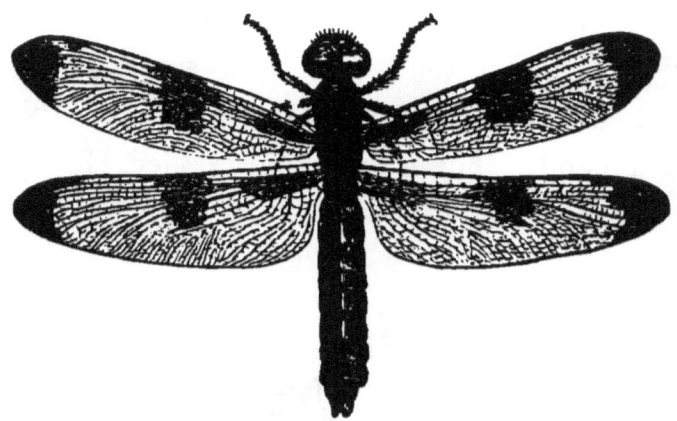

A Dragon-Fly, — a Neuropter.

a long body. They are called Nerve-winged Insects, or Neuropters; and here is a picture of one of them.

THE BEES, WASPS, &c., or HYMENOPTERS.

The first story that I am going to tell you, is about the busy little Bees, — the honey-makers. They live together in very large numbers. In a single hive there are many thousands of these little creatures, and in every hive there are three kinds, the Queen, the Drones, and the Workers. Here are pictures of them. The Queen is the largest, — although her picture is no larger than that of the Drone, — and there is only one in each

The Queen. The Worker. The Drone.

hive. She is the mother; she lays all the eggs, and does not often fly out into the sunshine, but stays in the hive, and is fed and waited upon by the Workers. There are only a few Drones or males in each hive; they have no sting, and they do no work, and they do not often fly out of the hive. The Workers are the smallest; they make the comb, and fill it with honey which they gather from the flowers; they feed and take care of the young bees; they wait upon the Queen; they do all the work and are busy from morning till night.

The honeycomb is made of wax; you have often seen it, and you remember that it is made up of little cells, all shaped alike, each one having six sides; and the honey-cells are all of the same size, whether made by the honey-bees that live in our country, or by those that live in countries thousands of miles away, and whether made by the tame bees that live in hives, or by the wild bees that live in the forests, and have their nest and build their comb in hollow trees, or in holes and crevices among the rocks. The bottom of the cell is made of three " diamond " shaped pieces, and it is deepest in the centre, and is much stronger than if it were flat and made of only one piece. The bees begin at the top of the hive to make the comb, and build downward, each comb having two rows of cells, one tier or row of cells being open towards one side of the hive, the other tier or row of the same comb being open towards the opposite side of the hive. When the bees have filled the honey-cells they close the top with wax, and the honey is thus kept from the air, and it remains pure and sweet.

But you will like to know more about the wax, for it is a very wonderful substance, and the way in which it is formed is very curious. On the under side of the hind body of the bee are six little flaps, or pockets, and under these flaps the wax is secreted, in tiny scales; and, in order to produce it, the bees must have plenty of food, and then they must keep warm and quiet for about a day; so the little wax-makers first eat all the honey or sugar they need, and then they arrange themselves in the form of festoons and curtains, — by clinging one to another with the claws of their feet, while the first and last bees attach themselves to some part of the hive or comb, — and in this way they hang until the wax is secreted, and then they go to that part of the comb where wax is needed, and by means of the pincers of their legs they remove the little scales of wax, and mould and work them over with the head and tongue, softening them with a frothy liquid from the mouth. The wax is formed so slowly that it is a very precious substance, and it is a very curious fact that the shape of the bee's cell is such as to use as little as possible, and still have the cells and comb firm and strong. Although when warm the wax is soft and can be moulded and spread into any form, when cold it is hard and firm enough to bear the weight of the young bees and the honey; and the texture of this wonderful substance is so close that, although the walls of the cells are very thin and delicate, not a particle of honey can soak through them.

After the wax has served its purpose for the bee, it is useful to man in many ways. It is made into beautiful candles for lighting churches and dwellings; the thread with which we sew is made smoother and stronger by it; the prettiest dolls are made of wax; and it is used in making the beautiful wax fruits and flowers which look so nearly like real fruits and flowers.

The bees also collect the gum which comes from the poplar, birch, willow, and other trees, and from this gum they form a substance called propolis; this is harder and firmer than wax, and the bees use it to strengthen the cells, and sometimes to fasten the comb to the top of the hive; it is also used to close all the cracks and holes in the hive where rain might come in, or where insects or snails might enter.

Bees also gather the pollen or yellow dust of

flowers, and they have, on the last pair of legs, two little cavities, or "baskets," in which they carry it to the hive, where it is mixed with honey and made into a substance called "bee-bread." This "bee-bread" is used mainly for food for the young bees. Bees have been watched while gathering pollen, and it is said that from whatever kind of flower they begin to gather the pollen, they keep on gathering from the same kind until they fill their baskets and are ready to return with it to the hive; and that they do this even when many other kinds of flowers are all about them.

The air inside of a bee-hive, where so many little creatures are busily at work, is always warm, but the bees have a curious way of lessening the heat, and keeping the air pure. If you have ever been near a hive, you may have seen, just in front of the entrance, rows of bees swiftly moving their wings as though they were fanning; and if you have looked within the hive, you have seen other rows of bees near the entrance, fanning in the same way; this fanning keeps the air in motion, so that currents of cool air are all the time going in, and currents of warmer air are all the time passing out. If it were not for this, the air within the hive would get so heated that the wax would soften, and the combs would fall. This sometimes happens in very warm weather, in spite of all the bees can do to keep the hive cool, and then they get very angry, and sting any one who comes near them.

Perhaps you would like to know more about the sting of the bee, and how so small an insect is able to hurt you so much. The sting consists of a hollow and sharp-pointed tube, or sheath, within which are two minute darts, which are hooked at the end, and the sheath connects with a bag of poison within the body of the bee. When the bee is angry, it thrusts the sheath into your hand, or whatever it wishes to sting; the darts are pushed through the sheath, and the poison flows into the wound thus made.

But I must tell you about the young bees. In some of the cells the Queen lays her eggs, one in each cell, and in a few days these eggs hatch into little soft, white, worm-like creatures, which are taken care of and fed by the Workers. In five or six days more the Workers close the top of each cell, and the little larva, or worm-like creature, thus shut in, soon begins to spin a silken covering around itself, which it completes in one or two days. This silken cover is called a cocoon, from a word which means a shell. In this shell, or cocoon, the young bee remains a week or more, until it is ready to come forth a perfect bee. It then bites a hole in the top of the cell, crawls out of its little nest, and, in a day or two, if it is a Working Bee, it is flying over the fields in search of honey.

Among the cells for eggs there are always a few that are made larger than the others, and they are of a different shape; these are for the young Queens, and they are called Royal Cells. When the eggs in these cells are hatched, the little larvæ are fed with a different and better kind of food, and they grow into young Queens. Now, when a young Queen crawls out of her cell, and appears in the hive, the old Queen seems to be very angry, and, if she could get at the young Queen, she would sting her to death. But the young Queen is carefully guarded by some of the Workers, until it is known whether the old Queen will depart with a swarm. Perhaps you do not know what is meant by a swarm of bees. I will tell you. When a great many bees have been hatched, and the hive is not large enough for all of them to live in it, and work together, the old Queen leaves the hive and is followed by many of the Drones and Workers; this is called swarming. When the Queen alights, the other bees alight upon and around her, making sometimes a bunch of bees as large as a man's head. Now if the old Queen is going to leave the hive, the young Queen will be needed, and this is the reason why she is guarded so carefully. If the old Queen does not leave in a day or two, the two Queens are allowed to come near each other, and begin the fight which does not end until one of them kills the other.

Every boy whose home is in the country knows what it is to hunt for the nests of the Humble-bees, for these bees build in the ground, or under stones, or in the little nests of grass that the field-mice have made and left. The Humble-bees are much larger than the Honey-Bees, but they do not live together in such large numbers; in some nests there are not more than fifty or sixty bees, but sometimes there are as many as three hundred, or even four hundred in the same family. In each nest there are four kinds, — the large females, the males, the workers, and the small females. In the autumn, all, except the large females, die; these stay in a sort of chamber near the nest, which is made soft and warm with moss and grass, or they crawl into some sheltered spot under a stone, or a stump, or among the dry leaves, and there sleep until the warm sunny days of spring have come; then each one begins to seek a spot in which to make her nest. When the bee has found a place to suit her, she begins to collect pollen and honey, which she brings to her nest, and when she has a little mass of it, she lays in it several eggs; these soon hatch, and the young ones feed upon the pollen, and grow quite fast, and when they get their full size each one spins around itself a silken cocoon, which the old bee covers with wax. In these cells they remain until they change into perfect bees, and then they bite their way out. While these little bees have been growing, the old bee has gathered other masses of pollen and honey in which she has laid more eggs, so that little broods of bees are every week or two hatching out. The first broods are all workers. The small females and males are produced about the middle of summer; and from the last eggs which are laid come the large females or queens, which live through the winter and found new colonies the next spring.

The bees which I have been telling you about are called Social-Bees, because they live and work together in families; but there are other kinds of bees that live alone, each one making her own nest, and these are called Solitary-Bees. One kind bores into wood to make her nest, and from this she is called the Carpenter-Bee. She has strong jaws, with which she bites out the wood, and the hole that she makes is a foot or more in length. It takes the little bee many days to do this. When she has made it deep enough, she begins to collect pollen and honey which she carries in, and when she has gathered a little mass of it, she lays an egg in it, and then begins to make a ceiling or roof so as to form a cell, for this long tube is divided into cells, each one of which is not quite an inch long. The ceiling or roof is made of the little chips and bits of wood and dust which the bee has taken out, and which she glues together with a sticky fluid from her body. When the ceiling is finished, she gathers more pollen and honey and lays another egg, and then makes a roof for this cell, and she keeps doing this until the whole tube is divided into cells. You may wonder how the bees get out, — since those in the lowest cells hatch first, — and I will tell you. Before she begins to fill the tube with cells the mother-bee makes a side opening near the bottom, and fills it with a dust paste; through this paste the first or lowest bee gnaws as soon as it is full grown, and the others follow in their turn.

Another kind of bee makes her cells of pieces of leaves, and she is called the Leaf-cutting, or Tailor-Bee. You may have seen leaves, and sometimes even the petals of flowers, which have been cut by this bee; she does this with her sharp jaws more neatly than you could do it with your scissors. It takes her only a few seconds to cut out a neat piece, such as she needs, and then she flies away with it, carrying it with her hind legs. As soon as the cell is done, she fills it with pollen, lays a single egg, then closes the top, and begins another cell; a single Leaf-cutter makes sometimes as many as thirty cells in one season. The egg soon hatches, and when the little larva has grown to its full size, it spins a silken case within its leafy cell, and by and by changes into a perfect bee, which bites its way out of its cell.

Another kind of bee makes her cells of mud, or of little grains of sand cemented together; and this kind is called the Mason-Bee.

Other kinds build under stones; others dig long tunnels in the ground; others burrow in the pithy stems of plants, and in the limbs of trees.

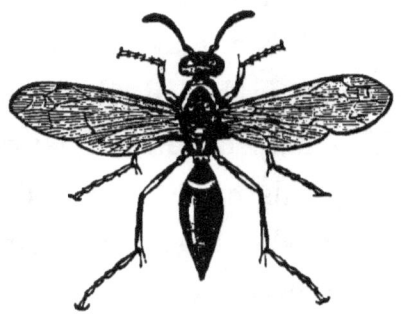

The Wasp.

Wasps eat other insects instead of feeding upon the sweet juices of flowers, and they do not make any honey, but they make very nice nests for their young ones to live in, and take good care of them so that I hope you will like to read about them. Some kinds live quite alone, each one building her own nest, but most kinds live together in large numbers, and in each nest there are males, females, and workers. They build their nests in the ground, or in holes, or on trees, bushes, fences, or buildings. You have seen these nests, and you remember that they are made of something which looks very much like paper; it is a sort of paper made of wood. The wasps gnaw the little woody fibres, and, with their jaws, soften them into a kind of paste, which hardens into paper. The wasps were truly the first paper-makers in the world! In the nest they build rows of cells of the same kind of paper, and in these cells the eggs are laid, and the young ones live and grow until they get to be perfect wasps. Some kinds of wasps build an open nest of only a few cells. Those called Mud-Wasps build their cells of mud, and after laying an egg in each cell, they fill the cells with insects and close the top. The insects are for the food of the young wasp. You have not forgotten, Amy, the two cells which one of these Mud-Wasps built last summer on the wall in the corner of the parlor. She worked very fast, and was only a few hours in building a cell. Flying out at the open window, she very soon returned with a ball of mud in her jaws, which she carried to the spot where she was building, placing and shaping it more neatly than you could have done it with your little hands. The day after she finished the first cell, she filled it with spiders, and closed the top with mud. While she was at work on the second cell, a gentleman got up to look at them more closely, and he broke a small piece out of the one which had been finished. As soon as she came in she saw the injury which had been done to her little cell, and immediately went to work to repair it, and in a very few minutes she had nicely mended it. Here is a picture of those little cells as they looked before the second one was filled with spiders and closed.

The Mud-Cells of the Mud-Wasp.

THE STORY OF THE COCOONS.

Almost every little girl and boy has seen the pretty yellow, silky cocoons that are made by the Tent-Caterpillar, or Apple-tree Worm as it is often called. Here is a picture of one of them, and of

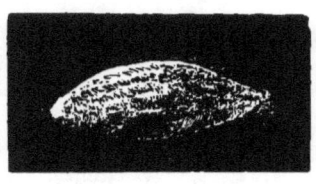

The Cocoon of the Tent-Caterpillar.

The Tent-Caterpillar Moth.

the pretty moth which comes out of it. A gentleman once put a large number of these cocoons into a box, hoping to have, in a week or two, many of these pretty moths. But when he opened the box he found only a few moths, and a large number of little insects which looked very much like the one whose picture you see here.

You will like to know the name of these little insects, and how they got into the box, for it had been tightly closed all of the time. I will tell you. They are Ichneumons. That word looks as though it might not be easy for you to pronounce it, but you will find that it is not any longer than the word "butterfly," and I presume you never think that "butterfly" is a hard word to speak. The eggs from which these little insects hatched were laid by the mother Ichneumon in the body of the Apple-tree Caterpillar, perhaps before it spun its little cocoon, perhaps not till after the cocoon was made; for Ichneumons always lay their eggs either in, or upon, other insects, or in the eggs of other insects, and when the young Ichneumon hatches, it begins to eat up the insect in which it finds itself. This is just what those little fellows in the box had done; they had eaten the caterpillars that were inside the cocoons, and, when they had grown large enough, they made their own little cocoons inside of the larger silky ones, and after a while they came out as perfect little Ichneumons.

Some kinds of Ichneumons are much larger than those I have just been telling you about, and they have, on the hind part of the body, a very long piercer, composed of three bristle-like parts, with which they lay their eggs in deep holes. Here is a picture of one of the large ones laying her

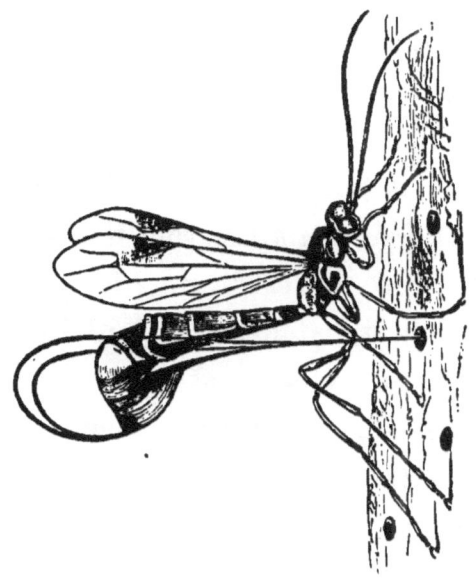

The Ichneumon.

eggs. The holes are made in the trunk of a tree by the Boring Saw-Fly, for its own eggs, and after they are laid, the Ichneumon comes and lays its eggs in those of the Boring Saw-Fly. I will show you a picture of the Saw-Fly by and by, and will then tell you something more about it.

Sometimes you will see little bunches growing

on the leaves and stems of plants. These are called galls. Perhaps you have seen the oak-apples, or oak-galls that grow on the leaves and twigs of the oak-tree. They are not like the apples that grow on the apple-tree, and if you should cut one of them open, you would find, in the inside, a little white worm-like creature. How do you think it got in there? There is no hole in the gall, and so you know that it has not crawled in. It has lived there all its life, and the little egg from which it hatched was laid by the mother when the leaf or stem was green and smooth. After the egg is laid, all this bunch grows around it; and when the little insect hatches, it has all this to feed upon, and when it has grown large and strong enough, it gnaws its way out of the gall. There are many kinds of these little gall-flies, and the galls that they make differ very much from one another. Some kinds of galls are shaped like an apple; others like a bunch of currants; some are almost as hard as a stone, and others are as juicy as fruit. Some kinds of galls are very useful. The ink which we write with is made out of galls caused by a little gall-fly which lives on the oak-trees that grow in Western Asia. Here is a picture of a little Gall-Fly which lives on

The Rose-Bush Gall-Fly.

rose-bushes, but you must not think that it is as large as you see it here. The straight black mark or line that you see near the picture shows you the length of the little insect itself. If you look on the stems of the rose-bushes, you will sometimes find long woody bunches or galls growing firmly to the stems; it is in these that the Rose-bush Gall-Flies live while they are in the young state.

On the next page there is a picture of the Boring Saw-Fly of which I told you in the story of the Ichneumon. It is a large black and yellow insect, and looks a little like a very large wasp or hornet, with a very long sting. But what you see is not a sting; it is only the hard pointed end of the body, and under it is the borer with which the insect makes holes in the trunks of trees in which to lay its eggs. These eggs hatch into little white grubs, which feed upon the wood of the tree, and when large enough each one makes a little cocoon of

The Tremex, or Boring Saw-Fly.

silk and chips of wood in which it stays for a long time. When its wings have fully grown, and it is ready to come out, it breaks through its cocoon, crawls to the opening of its burrow, gnaws through the bark and flies out into the air.

You have seen a carpenter at work with his

saw, and you know how quickly he can cut a board, or even a large stick of wood, into pieces; but perhaps you do not know that some of the little insects have saws, which they use to cut holes and slits in the leaves and branches of trees, and other plants, in which to lay their eggs. Such insects are called Saw-Flies. Here is a picture of one. This one is only about a quarter

The Saw-Fly.

of an inch long, but it is drawn large so that you may see its form better than you could if it were made just as large as it really is. You cannot see its two little saws, for they are on the under part of the body, but I will tell you about them. When not in use they lie in a deep groove on the under part of the hind body, and are covered by two pieces which serve as a sheath, but they are so fixed to the body of the little creature that she can draw them out of the groove and move them up and down, whenever she wishes to use them. Each one, like the carpenter's fine saw, has a back to keep it steady, and, besides being toothed on the edge, it is covered, on one side, with rows of very fine teeth, so that it is a rasp as well as a saw. The little insect moves these saws up and down, first one and then the other, until she makes a slit deep enough for her eggs.

The young Saw-Flies look very much like small caterpillars; they live upon and eat the leaves of plants. Some kinds live alone, other kinds live together in swarms under silken webs which they spin to shelter them. Other kinds live in swarms, but without any web over them, and when they are disturbed they curl themselves up into very curious shapes. Many of them go into the ground to make their little silken cocoons; some kinds make them under leaves and stones, and others fasten them to the plants on which they live. Most of them stay in their cocoons all winter, and the next spring they come out perfect little Saw-Flies.

THE SCALY-WINGED INSECTS, or LEPIDOPTERS.

This is the picture of a little worm-like animal which you can find almost any day in summer

The Caterpillar, or Larva, of the Asterias Butterfly.

on the parsnip or the carrot bed in the garden. But this picture does not show you its fine colors; it is bright green, with bands of black and yellow spots, and it is very handsome. If you touch this little creature, it pushes out from its head two soft yellow horns. It is often called the Parsnip-Worm. But we will not call it a worm, for it is not one; it is a caterpillar. Would you like to know why it is called a caterpillar instead of a worm? It is because that by and by it will become a butterfly. A worm is never anything more than a worm, but all caterpillars are either baby-butterflies or baby-moths; and all of our beautiful moths and butterflies were once caterpillars living upon plants and eating leaves, instead of flying about and feeding upon the sweet honey of the flowers. If you could watch this caterpillar you would find that after a few weeks it leaves the plants upon which it has been feeding, and crawls away to some sheltered spot on the side of a building or fence, or the trunk of a tree. Here it spins a little tuft of silk. I think you will like to know how it is that the caterpillar can spin this beautiful silk, and I will tell you. Within its body are two long bags which hold a sticky fluid; these bags connect with a little tube which ends in the middle of the lower lip of the caterpillar. Now, when the caterpillar wishes to spin, he makes this fluid flow out of the little tube, and as soon as it comes to the air it hardens into a silken thread; and all the silk used for sewing, for fringes and tassels, for pretty ribbons, and for beautiful dresses, comes from the cocoons or silken shells which caterpillars spin around themselves. The caterpillar that I have been telling you about does not make a cocoon, but after it has spun its tuft of silk, it fixes the little claws of its hind feet in it, and then spins a loop of many silken threads, which it fastens at both ends to the board or tree on which it is spinning; when the caterpillar has made the loop strong enough, it passes its head under and works the loop over its back, so as to hold its body firmly, and keep it from falling. In a few hours its caterpillar skin bursts open and falls off, and then the little animal looks just as you see it in this picture. It is now called a

The Chrysalis of the Asterias Butterfly.

chrysalis. And here it hangs about two weeks, eating nothing, and not moving unless touched; but in twelve or fourteen days the chrysalis skin bursts open on the back, and a beautiful Butterfly comes forth. At first it is soft and weak, and it clings to the empty shell, but its little limbs soon become firm, its wings expand, and it flies away to feed upon the honey of flowers. Here is a picture of it as it now looks. It is black, with yellow, blue, and orange spots, and you can scarcely believe that it is the same insect that you first saw on the parsnip plants.

The Asterias Butterfly.

It does not grow any larger, for it is full-grown when it comes out of its chrysalis skin, but it flies about and soon lays its eggs on those plants that the caterpillars like to eat, and where they will find plenty of food as soon as they are hatched. By the time that the second brood of caterpillars has gone into the chrysalis form, it is late in the fall, so they hang through all the winter, and come forth butterflies the next summer.

The beautiful yellow and black butterfly, which you see in the warm sunny days of June and July, is one of the largest in our country. It is so shy that you cannot often get near it. Some times it flies very high in the air, above the houses, and even the tall trees, so that, if you were not looking sharply, you might suppose it to be a pretty yellow bird, instead of a delicate butterfly. When it is a caterpillar it lives upon the apple and wild-cherry trees, and feeds upon their leaves, and it has such a curious way of hiding that I must tell you about it. On the upper part of the leaf it spins a little web of silk, and folds over the edges of the leaf, and fastens them with silken threads so as to make a little case for itself. I will tell you what its colors are, so that you may know it when you find it. It is green with rows of blue dots, and yellow and black marks, and its head and legs are of a pink color. Early in the month of August it becomes a chrysalis, first hanging itself up by the little claws of its hind feet, and it comes forth as a butterfly the next summer. You may see its picture on the next page.

42 PICTURES AND STORIES OF ANIMALS.

The Yellow and Black Butterfly, or Turnus Butterfly.

THE WHITE AND THE YELLOW BUTTERFLY.

In May and June, and in July and August, you may see the beautiful White Butterfly near the growing mustard, radishes, turnips, and cabbage; it is then laying its eggs on these plants. It fastens them to the under side of the leaves, and lays but a few on each leaf. These eggs hatch in about ten days, and the caterpillars which come from them feed upon the leaves, and grow to their full size, of about one inch and a half in length, in three weeks. When they are full grown, they leave the plants and go among the rocks, or into cracks in boards or timber, and each one spins a little tuft of silk; into this tuft it fixes its hindmost feet, and then spins a loop to hold up the fore part of the body. Having done this it casts off its caterpillar skin and becomes a chrysalis. It stays in the chrysalis state about eleven days, and then comes forth as the beautiful White Butterfly.

There is another butterfly that is more common than the one of which I have just told you. It is the Colias, or the Common Yellow Butterfly. You will see it early in the spring, and until June, in the fields and by the roadside. Sometimes you will find many butterflies of this kind sitting around a pool of water in the street. When you come near them they all fly away, but sometimes come back again when you are gone. When in the caterpillar state the Yellow Butterflies are green, and live upon the growing clover plants. I must tell you that a second brood of the Yellow Butterflies appear about the first of August, and these are seen in the fields till late in the autumn.

There are many other beautiful butterflies which we see in our gardens, and in the clover-fields, and wherever there are blossoms. I wish I had pictures of them all to show you; but I have not, and so I must ask you to look for them in the fields and meadows, and watch them there, and that will be even better than seeing pictures of them.

The butterflies whose pictures I have now shown you have the hind wings extended into a sort of tail; but the White Butterfly and the Yellow Butterfly, and many others, — a few of which I will tell you of, — have the wings rounded as you see them in the pictures on the next two pages.

The Misippus Butterfly is of a yellowish-brown or tawny yellow color, with black stripes, and a black border, and the black border is spotted with

The Misippus Butterfly.

white. The caterpillar eats the leaves of the poplar and of the willow.

The butterflies whose pictures I have now shown you, and about which you have been reading, live in the fields and meadows, and in the orchards and gardens, and we may see some of them every pleasant day in summer; but on the next page there is a picture of a butterfly which lives upon the high mountains, and it has been named the Mountain Butterfly. It has been found only on Mount Washington, the highest of the White Mountains, — a wild and very interesting region in New Hamp-

The Mountain Butterfly.

shire, which you will like to visit when you are older.

The Skipper Butterflies are so called because they fly only a little way at a time, and with a

The Skipper.

skipping, jerking motion. You will see them in every grassy field, and in the meadow, and often about low bushes and thickets. They are of different colors, but many of them are brown and yellow. The caterpillars live quite alone, often hiding in folded leaves held together by silken threads.

I will now tell you about the Moths, and I think you would first like to know the difference between a moth and a butterfly.

The Butterflies fly in the daytime, and when they alight on the ground, or on a plant, and are at rest, they hold their wings erect, as you see them in the picture of the Mountain Butterfly; and the little feelers which grow out of the head are slender, and at the end of these there is a knob, and their caterpillars do not make the beautiful silky cocoons that I have told you about.

The Moths fly mostly at night and at twilight, and when they alight, and are at rest, they have their wings flat, or sloping like a roof, as you

A Moth.

see them in this picture, and their feelers have no knob at the end. The caterpillars of many of the moths make silken cocoons.

On the next page there is a picture of a large and beautiful moth, which is often seen at twilight hovering over the flowers of the garden, pushing its long tongue into the petunias, and other sweet blossoms, and darting from flower to flower as swiftly as the humming-bird. Sometimes it is called the Humming-bird Moth, because the noise which it makes with its wings when it is flying sounds like that which the humming-bird makes when it is fluttering around the flowers; and sometimes it is called the Hawk-Moth, because it

The Larva, or Caterpillar of the Five-spotted Sphinx.

hovers over the flowers somewhat as a hawk hovers over the little animal which he is about to dart down upon. Its wings are of a mingled black and gray color, and on each side of its body are five orange-colored spots, and from these it gets

THE FIVE-SPOTTED SPHINX, OR HAWK MOTH.

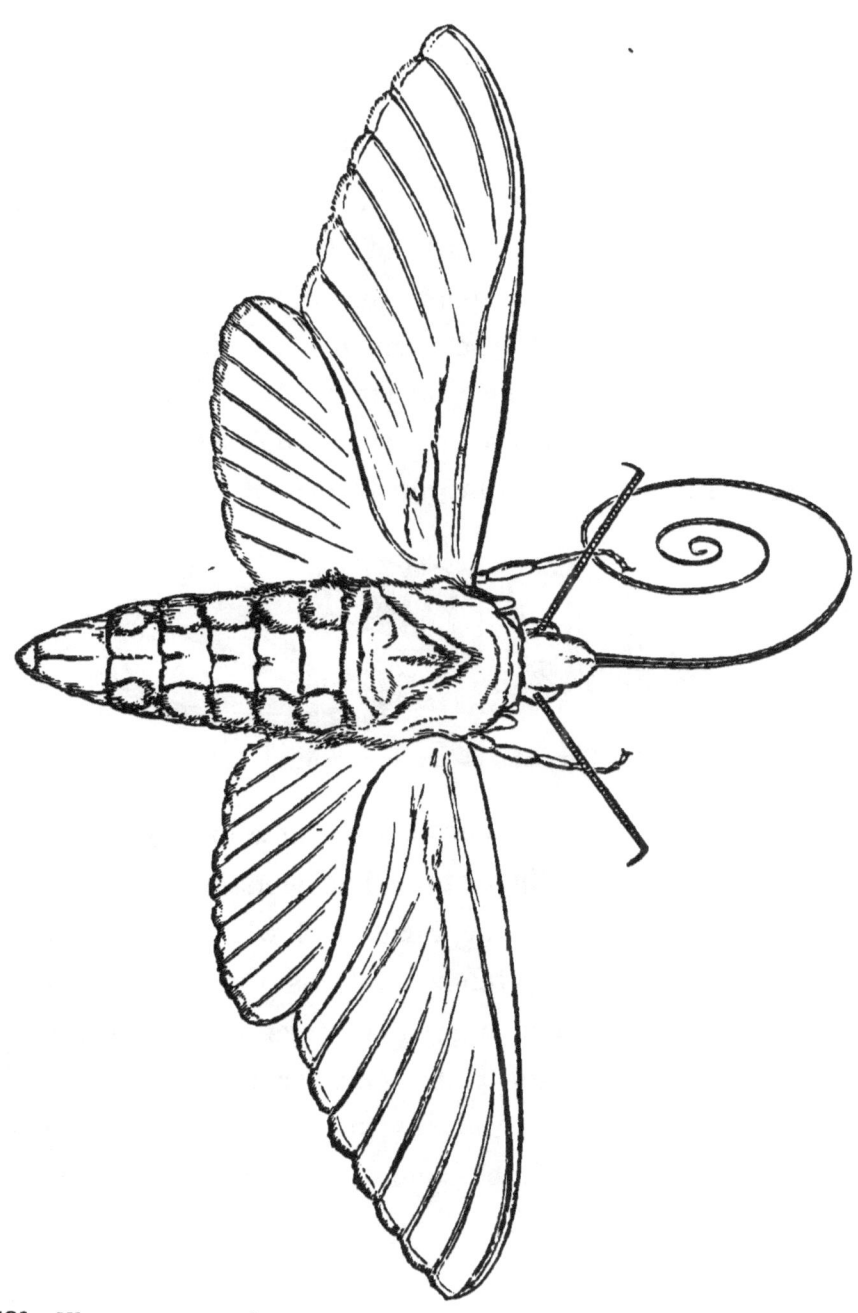

The Five-spotted Sphinx, or Hawk Moth.

the name of Five-spotted Sphinx. The caterpillar lives on the potato-plants and is called the "potato-worm." It is of a light green color, with white stripes on the sides, and a sort of thorn on the tail. In the month of August it gets to its full size, and is about three inches long. It then crawls down the stem of the plant on which it has been feeding, buries itself in the ground, and in a few days it throws off its caterpillar skin and becomes a bright brown chrysalis. Here

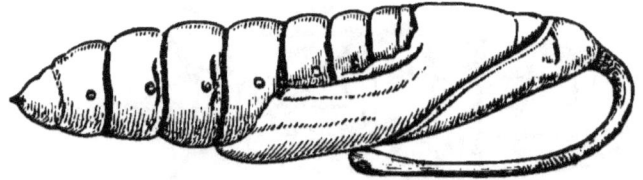

The Chrysalis of the Five-spotted Sphinx.

is a picture which shows you how it looks when it is in its chrysalis form. The slender part which is bent over from the head, and which looks like the handle of a pitcher, contains the long tongue of the moth. The chrysalis stays in the ground all winter, and the next summer the large moth crawls out of it, comes to the top of the ground, and if it is daytime, conceals itself under leaves or in some quiet spot, and waits until evening, when it flies away in search of honey, which is its food.

The Clear-winged Sesia.

This moth has beautiful transparent wings and a broad fan-shaped tail, and it flies about in the brightest sunshine, instead of in the evening, and as it hovers over the flowers it looks so much like a little humming-bird, that it is sometimes called the Humming-Bird Moth. Another name for it is Clear-winged Sesia. You will sometimes see this pretty moth feeding upon the sweet blossoms of the phlox, and you will like to watch it as it flies from flower to flower. It does not alight upon the flowers, but it poises itself above them, keeping its wings in rapid motion all of the time.

This little moth is blue and yellow, and it looks very much like a small wasp. When it is a cater-

The Peach-tree Borer.

pillar it lives in the trunk of the peach-tree, and feeds upon the wood, and so it is called the Peach-tree Borer. The moth lays its eggs on the trunk of the tree, generally near the roots, and the little caterpillars gnaw through the bark into the tree, and there they live for about a year. They often injure the tree so much that it cannot bear fruit, and sometimes they gnaw quite around it, and thus cause it to die. They make their little cocoons just under the bark, or in the earth close to the roots of the tree. Sometimes this little moth lays its eggs on the cherry-trees.

In the last part of summer, you may perhaps find in the fields the beautiful moth whose picture you see upon the next page. Its fore wings are yellow, with six white stripes on each, and on the white stripes are little dots of black; the hind wings are of a bright scarlet color with a wide irregular border of black. It is one of the prettiest

The Beautiful Deïopeia.

moths that you will ever see, and its name is Beautiful Deïopeia. The caterpillar of this little moth is said to feed upon the leaves of the blue lupine and the wild forget-me-not.

You have often seen in summer a caterpillar thickly covered with short, stiff, and even hairs, which are black on the four forward rings, and on the two hind rings, and tan-red on those between. If this caterpillar be handled, it at once curls up into a ball. But I do not want you to handle it, as the stiff hairs may injure your fingers. In the autumn it crawls under a board or a stone, where it sleeps all winter. In the spring it makes a blackish cocoon, and in the summer comes out a moth of a tawny color, with a few black spots on the wings, and a row of black dots on each side and above the body.

The salt-marshes, or lowlands near the sea, are sometimes thickly inhabited by caterpillars, which eat the grass, and in this way do much injury to the owners of the marshes, who wish to cut the grass and make hay of it. Here is a picture of one of these caterpillars. In the

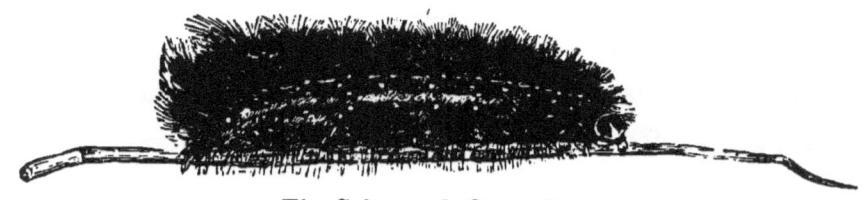

The Salt-marsh Caterpillar.

month of August the Salt-marsh Caterpillars are full grown, and then they sometimes leave the marshes and go on the higher lands so as to make their cocoons in those places that cannot be reached by the high tides. They hide in hay-stacks and wood-piles, under stones and in walls, where they make coarse hairy cocoons, and then change to chrysalids. Sometimes they remain on the marshes, and make their cocoons under the coarse grass and stubble. Here is a picture of the little chrysalis which is inside of the cocoon. After

The Salt-marsh Moth and Chrysalis.

staying in this form through all the cold winter, it comes forth the next June a beautiful moth with white fore wings, and yellow hind ones, and all spotted with black. In the warm summer evenings, when the windows are open, and the lamps are lighted, these pretty moths fly into the room and dart about the flame until their wings are so burned that they can fly no more.

But I must tell you about the Silk-worm,— the caterpillar from which comes almost all the silk used in the world. The egg from which it is hatched is about as large as a mustard-seed, and the little creature is at first only about one tenth of an inch in length. It grows very fast, for it spends almost all the time in eating, except when it is about to shed its skin. Like all other caterpillars, it sheds its skin several times before it reaches its full growth. It feeds upon the leaves of the mulberry-tree, and during its caterpillar life it eats many thousand times its own weight. When full-grown it is about three inches in length, and its color is pale green, with darker marks, and its head is black. When ready to make its cocoon, the people who take care of these little creatures almost always place near each one of them a twig, or a rolled paper, or something hollow, into which it can crawl, and to which it may attach its silken threads. It first spins a loose covering of silk; within this it spins a finer silk, the threads of which it glues together with a sort of gum; and the inside is lined with more delicate silk glued more firmly together; and thus the little chrysalis within the cocoon is sheltered from rain, wind, and cold. The cocoon is from an inch to an inch and a half in length, and it is of a yellow color. When the cocoon is finished, the caterpillar changes to a chrysalis, and remains in this state from two to eight weeks. In warm countries, or in warm rooms, the moth comes forth much sooner than it does in cooler climates, or when kept in cool rooms. The color of the moth is grayish or yellowish white. This insect, so useful to man, was known in China more than four thousand years ago. From China it has been carried to many other countries, and it is now raised in vast numbers in Italy, France, Spain, Russia, and in other parts of the world; and many thousands of people are employed in feeding and taking care of the caterpillars, and winding the silk from the cocoons, and getting it ready to be woven into ribbons, and webs of silk, satin, and velvet.

A great many years ago silk was thought, by some people, to be a downy fleece which grew upon trees, and it was worth its weight in gold; it was sometimes woven with threads of gold, and often beautifully embroidered with gold. It was so rare and costly an article that even an Emperor refused his Empress a garment of silk, because it was so expensive! It is now so common that it is worn in some form by almost every person.

I want to tell you about the large silk-worm moths which live in the woods and groves of our country. There are several kinds whose caterpillars make large silky cocoons, but, so far as we know, only one of these makes cocoons which can be easily unwound. The moth is so large and so handsome, and its habits are so interesting, that I must tell all about it, and show you a picture of the caterpillar, and the cocoon, and the chrysalis, and also a picture of the great moth itself. A gentleman, M. Trouvelot, living in Medford, Massachusetts, has been studying and raising this moth for more than six years, and he has told us many new and interesting facts about it. The caterpillar is of a beautiful light

The American Silk-Worm.

green color, with pale yellow lines on its sides, and on every ring of its body are little warts, or tubercles, of a lustre like pearl, and tinged with orange, red, or purple. The large green caterpillar which we found under the oak-tree last autumn was one of this kind, and you will remember, Amy, how beautiful it was in the evening; for then some of the spots shone like gold, others were rosy-red, while the body of the insect was of a clear pale-green color. The caterpillar likes to eat the leaves of the oak-tree, and it also eats the leaves of the elm, willow, birch, poplar, maple, and the leaves of the hazel and blueberry, and of other plants. By the time it is full-grown, M. Trouvelot says it has eaten not less than one hundred and twenty oak leaves. When ready to make

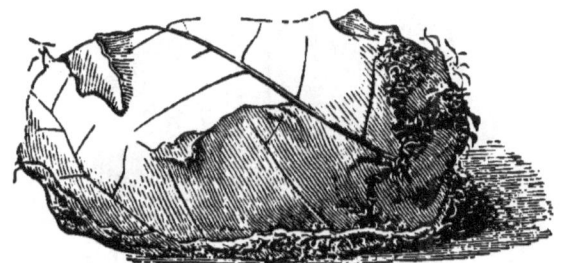

The Cocoon of the American Silk-Worm.

its cocoon, it first spins silken threads from one leaf to another, until it has drawn three or four leaves around itself in such a manner that they will enclose and partly conceal its cocoon; it then spins between these leaves in every direction until it is surrounded by silken threads, and within these it spins layers of silk which it glues together with a sort of gummy, sticky substance, and in this way the cocoon is made strong and firm. The cocoon is only about half as large as the caterpillar is when it begins to spin, and at first you can scarcely believe that it contains the insect; but the caterpillar becomes smaller by spinning, for the silk is a fluid which flows out of its body. In four or five days the cocoon is finished, and the caterpillar changes to a

The Chrysalis of the American Silk-Worm after the Cocoon is taken off.

chrysalis, and remains in this state all winter, sometimes frozen as hard as a stone. The next

THE AMERICAN SILK-WORM MOTH.

The American Silk-worm Moth, or Polyphemus Moth.

summer, in June, the large and beautiful moth comes forth. The moth lays its eggs on the under side of the oak leaves, and one moth lays three hundred or more.

All of these pictures of the American Silk-Worm — the caterpillar, the cocoon, the chrysalis, and the moth itself — are from "The American Naturalist," a beautiful and interesting magazine of Natural History, published by the Peabody Academy of Science, at Salem, Massachusetts.

Another large moth, of which I wish to tell you, is the Luna, or the "Pale Empress of the Night." Its wings expand four or five inches, and the hind ones are extended into a long tail. The wings are of a delicate light-green color, and on each one there is an eye-like spot which is clear in the centre and surrounded by rings of white, red, yellow, and black. In the caterpillar state it lives on trees, especially the walnut-trees, and in July and August it is two or three inches in length, and is then bluish-green, with a yellow stripe on each side of the body, and yellow bands on the back between the rings. On each ring there are about six pearly-colored warts, tinged with purple, and at the end of the body there are three brown spots with a yellow border above. When it is ready to go into the chrysalis state, it draws together two or three leaves, and spins its cocoon inside of them. The cocoon falls with the leaves in the autumn, and the next June the beautiful Luna Moth comes forth from its silken covering where it has stayed during all the winter.

Another moth of which I wish to tell you is the Cecropia. Its wings expand over six inches, and are of a dusky brown color, with clay-colored hind margins, and near the middle of each wing there is a large reddish spot with a white centre and a narrow black edging, and beyond the spot a reddish band with a white border on the inside. You may find this magnificent moth in the groves and near the borders of woods, in the early part of summer. The caterpillar is three inches long, of a light-green color, and has red and yellow warts armed with short bristles. It fastens its large cocoon to the side of a stem or twig.

The large and beautiful Moth called the Promethea, has its wings brown with a drab border, and very prettily marked with wavy

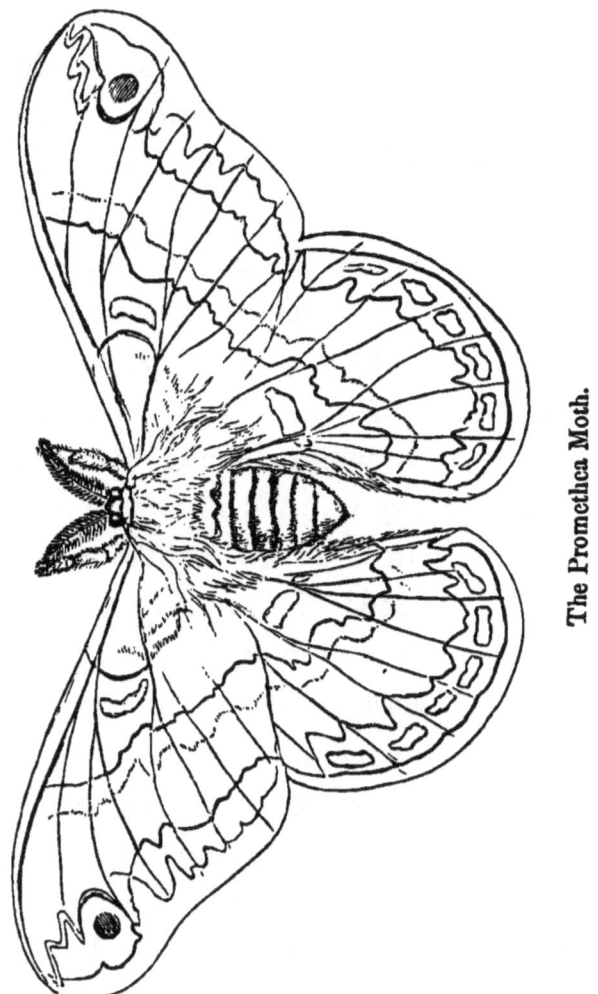

The Promethea Moth.

lines of red and white. The caterpillar lives upon the sassafras-tree, and it is pale green with yellow feet, head, and tail, and its body is marked with red, yellow, and blue warts. Before making the cocoon, in which it is to stay all winter, the caterpillar fastens to the twig, with many silken threads, the leaf that is to cover its cocoon, so that it may not fall to the ground in autumn, with the other leaves; then it spins its cocoon on the leaf, bending over the edges so as to cover and conceal it, and there it safely swings through all the storms and winds of winter. If you are walking in the woods late in the autumn, or in the winter, you may, perhaps, find some of these cocoons, and if you take them home and keep them until the next July, you will have the pleasure of seeing these beautiful moths when they come out of their cocoons, and before they have been injured by flying about among the trees and bushes.

You have seen the large tent-like nests that are sometimes made on apple-trees, and on wild-cherry trees; they are called Worms'-nests, but they are made by the Tent-Caterpillar. The Moth lays her eggs on the branches of these trees, and covers them with a sort of varnish which makes them water-proof, for they are to remain on the trees through the autumn rains and winter snows. In the early part of summer, about the time the leaves begin to unfold, these eggs hatch into little caterpillars, which soon begin to make a silken nest, or tent, between the forks of the branches, and as they grow they make the tent larger by spinning new layers of silk. They go out of the tent to feed twice every day, once in the forenoon, and once in the afternoon, and return to their nest when they have finished eating. In crawling from one twig to another they spin a thread of silk, so that, by following the thread, they may be able to find the way back to their nest. When they have eaten all of the leaves on the tree, they crawl down the trunk, spinning as they go, and feed upon the plants that grow near the tree, and you may sometimes see the grass around the roots of the tree covered by their silken threads. Sometimes when another tree is near, they crawl to that and feed upon its leaves. They stay in their webs or tents at noon, and in stormy weather. When they have grown to their full size, they leave the trees, and wander about for a little while, but soon, in some sheltered spot, they spin their pretty little cocoons, and in about twelve or fifteen days the moths come forth, and in the warm summer

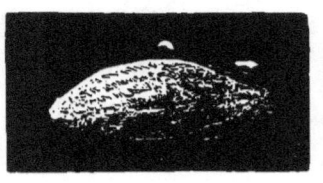

The Cocoon of the Tent-Caterpillar.

The Tent-Caterpillar Moth.

evenings they come in at the open windows and flit about the lights.

The Geometer, or Span-worm.

Many caterpillars, when they crawl, raise the middle of the body, as you see it in the picture; these are called Span-worms, or Measure-worms, because they seem to measure the ground over which they crawl. They cannot help moving in this way, for they have no legs on the midde of the body. They live upon trees, and let themselves down to the ground by a silken thread, which they spin from the mouth as they descend. When they are disturbed, they let themselves down and hang until all is quiet again, and then climb up by the same thread. The Canker-worms, which eat the leaves of our fruit and shade trees, are of this kind. About the time that the leaves of the apple-tree begin to start from the bud, the little caterpillars hatch from clusters of eggs which have been placed upon the trees by the moths. They immediately begin to eat, at first making only small holes in the leaves, but, as they grow, they enlarge these holes, until by and by little more is left than the veins of the leaves. In about four weeks they have grown to their full size, and they then spin their way down to the ground, into which they crawl and very soon go into the chrysalis form. They remain in the ground till after the autumn frosts, and then they begin to come out in the moth state whenever the weather is mild.

The Leaf-roller.

This little moth is one of the Leaf-rollers. You will like to know how it gets this name, and I will tell you. When it is a caterpillar it rolls up the edges of a leaf and fastens them with threads of silk, so as to make a little case in which it lives, and upon which it feeds. Other little caterpillars live in leaf and flower buds, fastening them with threads of silk so that they cannot open, and then they feed upon the tender leaves. The moths of these caterpillars are very small, and their fore wings are often prettily striped and banded, and sometimes they are adorned with little spots, which shine like silver and gold.

You have seen the little silvery-looking moths that fly about the rooms in early spring. They are so small that they can enter through cracks into closets, drawers, and chests, and they get under the edges of carpets, and into the folds of curtains

The Clothes Moth.

and lay their eggs, and the little caterpillars, as soon as they are hatched, begin to gnaw the carpet, clothes, curtains, or furs, or whatever they find themselves upon. Each one makes a little case for itself out of the cloth or fur on which it lives; this little case is open at both ends, and as the little fellow grows, and needs more room, he makes the case larger by cutting slits at the sides and weaving in more threads.

THE TWO-WINGED INSECTS, or DIPTERS.

I WILL now tell you about some little insects which have only two wings, but which have, in the place of the second pair of wings, two little knobbed threads called balancers, and just behind the two wings, and in front of the balancers, are two tiny scales, which open and shut with the motion of the wings; these are called winglets.

The wings of these insects are very thin and clear, and when the sun shines upon them they are very beautiful, often showing all the colors of the rainbow. Many of these little creatures can move their wings very swiftly, and in this way they make a buzzing or humming sound, which sometimes is not very pleasant to hear.

The most common of the two-winged insects, or dipters, as they are called,—a name which means two-winged, — are the Mosquitoes and the Flies. I will first tell you about the Mosquitoes. When young, they live in the water. You have often seen, in the summer-time, in pools, and in tubs and barrels of water, the little animals called "wrigglers"; these are young Mosquitoes, and if you have ever watched them, you know that they are very lively; they wriggle and tumble and twist about, and dive from time to time, then come to the top of the water to breathe, resting with the head downward; for at this time of their life they breathe through a little tube in the tail which ends in a feather-like tuft. In about two weeks they shed their skin, and although they still live in the water, their form is changed, and they now breathe through two little tubes upon the back. When it is time for the Mosquito to change into the winged form, it comes to the top of the water, and raises the middle portion of the body a little, the skin soon splits down the back, and the little creature quickly draws out its head and body, but still rests on its old skin, and floats about as though in a boat. The thin delicate wings soon unfold, and grow dry and firm, and the little insect flies away, happy in its new life, and ready to pierce men and animals for the blood upon which it delights to feed.

Mosquitoes and all other gnats — for Mosquitoes are one kind of gnat — are a very hungry and bloodthirsty race, and annoy us by their disagreeable hum and their poisonous bite. Their mouth is formed just right for the work which it has to do. It consists of a little sheath in which there are five slender bristles, sharper than the sharpest needles, with which they easily pierce our skin, and through which they suck our blood, first putting into the wound a poisonous fluid to make the blood thinner, and so cause it to flow more freely.

Some kinds of the two-winged insects, when in the grub or larva state, do much harm to the farmer by feeding upon the sap of the growing wheat. These are called Wheat-Flies and Hessian-Flies. They often move in great swarms, early in the morning, or just before night, in order to find the wheat-fields, and lay their eggs upon the growing grain. These flies are very small. The Hessian-Fly is no longer than the line which you see here beside its picture. It lays its eggs on the blades of the wheat, and in four or five days the eggs hatch; the young then crawl down

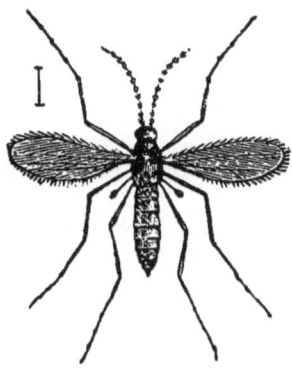

The Hessian-Fly.

the plant and fix themselves to its stem, just below the surface of the ground, and there feed upon its juices, and thus greatly injure, and sometimes kill, the tender plant. The Wheat-Fly is even smaller than the Hessian-Fly, and it lays its eggs in the blossoms of wheat and other grains, and the grubs or larvæ live in the heads of the grain, and feed upon the blossom and the growing tender kernel; they do not eat the kernel after it has become hard.

The Crane-Flies, or Harry-long-legs, have a long

body, and long legs which come off very easily. You may find these flies in the meadows, and sometimes they come in at the open window and rest upon the window-pane. When in the larva form some kinds live in the water; other kinds, when young, live in the ground and feed upon the roots of plants. A few days ago, a lady found in her hanging flower-basket a queer looking insect just coming out of its chrysalis skin. It was a Crane-Fly, which had been living upon the roots of her plants.

Many of the two-winged insects are very troublesome to men and animals. You have been bitten often enough by the mosquitoes to know how annoying they are. But the Black-Flies of the northern parts of our country and of Canada are even more troublesome than the mosquitoes. In June the air is filled with swarms of these insects, and hunters, and fishermen, and all who go into the woods, suffer greatly from their bites, which draw the blood and cause great irritation and pain. Later in the summer other kinds of flies come to take the places of the Black-Flies; these are so small that one can scarcely see them, and so the Indians of Maine call them the "no-see-um." The bite of these insects does not draw blood, but it causes a burning and smarting feeling like that caused by sparks of fire.

The Horse-Fly.   The Bee-Fly.

The Aslius-Fly.   The Bot-Fly.

There are many hundred kinds of flies. Some live in the house and are called House-Flies; these are very fond of sugar and all sweet food, and they have their mouth formed for lapping. Some kinds fly about the horses, and are called Horse-Flies; these pierce the skin with their sharp lancets, and suck the blood of the horse. Their eyes are very beautiful and very large also, making up nearly the whole of the head. Some flies when in the grub state live in the stomach of the horse; these are called Bot-Flies. Some kinds look like bees, and are called Bee-Flies; these live in the woods, and in the spring they are often seen in the sunny paths. They fly swiftly, but stop every little while and balance themselves in one place in the air. They often hover over the early flowers like humming-birds, and with their long bills suck out the sweet honey. Some flies have a very long body, and they catch and eat other insects; these are called the Asilus-Flies. When young they live in the roots of plants. One kind lives in the roots of the pie-plant, which you have often seen growing in the garden.

One of the most curious things about flies is, that they can run up and down window-panes, and along the ceiling, back downward, without any danger of falling. They can do this because on each foot, besides two hooks curved backward there are two minute flaps, or suckers, covered with the most delicate hairs, and these stick so closely to the surface of the pane or ceiling that they hold the fly and keep it from falling.

THE SHEATH-WINGED INSECTS, OR BEETLES.

Here are pictures of insects which are very different from those that you have been reading about. They have four wings, but the upper ones are hard and horn-like, while the under ones are thin, and when these insects are not flying, the

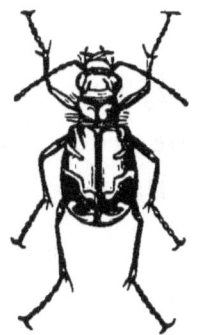

The Common Tiger Beetle.

The Hairy-necked Tiger Beetle.

thin under wings are folded up like a fan, and are hidden under the hard upper ones. They are called beetles; the word "beetle" means biter, and beetles have very strong jaws, with which they bite their food. When first hatched from the egg they are soft and worm-like, and are then called grubs. The colors of beetles are often very beautiful, and sometimes so brilliant that they shine like polished gold and precious stones. There are many thousand kinds of beetles, but in this little book you will see pictures of only a very few of them.

The two beetles whose pictures I have just shown you are called Tiger Beetles, and they are rightly named, for, like the tiger, they are not only very beautiful, but they are also very fierce. You will see them in warm sunny places, and in the roads in the country every pleasant summer day. As you come near them they fly quickly away, but soon alight again. Their little grubs have very strong jaws, and, like the beetles, they feed upon other insects. The grubs live in holes which they dig in the ground; when they are hungry, they come up so as to have the head just even with the top of the ground, and there they wait until some little insect passes by, when they seize him, drag him into the hole and eat him.

The Tiger Beetle Grub.

The Caterpillar-Hunter is of a bright shining green color, and it is very handsome. It does not fly, but it runs very rapidly. It is called the Caterpillar-Hunter, because it eats the young of other insects. It kills and eats great numbers of canker-worms, hunting them in the grass,

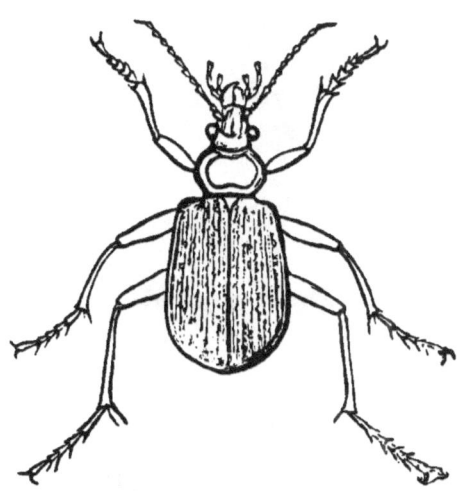

The Caterpillar-Hunter.

and even going up the trunks of the trees in order to catch them. It is therefore a very useful beetle, as it destroys insects which would injure our apple and shade trees.

If you take a fine net and dip it into the shallow waters of the pond, and move it around among the grass and weeds, and then take it from the water and carefully look at the things that are in it, you will find that you have caught several different kinds of animals, and among them you will sometimes find the curious Water Beetle, whose picture I here show you.

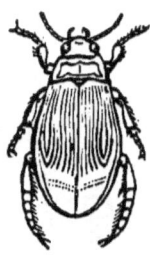

The Water Beetle.

The hind legs of this beetle are broad, and fringed with hairs, so that it can swim about very fast; it comes every few minutes to the top of the water to breathe, then darts away to catch and eat some water insect, or perhaps a young fish. The young or larva Water Beetle has a long body, six legs, and long, sharp, hooked jaws, that move sidewise, and it moves about swiftly in the water, and is a very hungry, savage creature, catching and killing small fishes and all other little water animals which it can master. After growing to its full size, and after shedding its skin several times, it creeps out of the water and digs a little hole in the bank of the pond, and there goes into the chrysalis state, and by and by it comes out a perfect Water Beetle.

Here is a picture of a large beetle which often flies in at the open window, in summer evenings

The Carrion Beetle.

when the lamps are lighted. You will know it by the color of its wings, which are black with orange-colored bands across them. It feeds upon the bodies of dead animals which it finds, and it is called the Carrion Beetle. Some kinds, when they find a dead bird, frog, or mouse, begin to dig the earth away under it, and keep at work until they sink the little animal out of sight; the eggs are then laid in the buried body, and when the young hatch, they find themselves in the midst of plenty of food suited to their wants.

This little beetle is found about decaying plants and animals. When you touch it, and when it

The Rove Beetle.

runs, it raises the hind body and moves it in different directions. It is called the Rove Beetle.

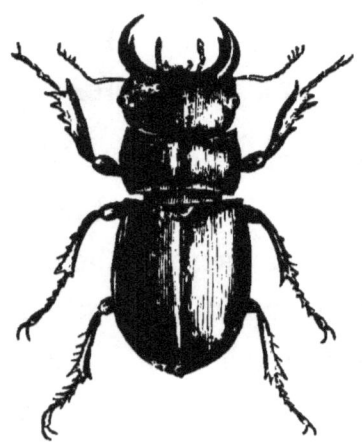

The Horn-Bug.

This beetle is called the Horn-Bug, or Stag Beetle, because its upper jaws are very long, curved, and branched like the horns of one kind of deer. We do not very often see it, for it stays in its hiding-places during the daytime, and flies about only at night. It feeds upon the sap of trees, and sometimes kills caterpillars and sucks out their juices. It lays its eggs in cracks in the bark of trees, often near the roots, and the grub lives in the trunk and roots five or six years before it becomes a perfect beetle.

The Goldsmith Beetle.

Here is a picture of one of the handsomest beetles in our country. On the upper side it is of a beautiful yellow color, and, when the sun shines upon it, it glistens like burnished gold; the under side is copper-colored, and covered with a whitish wool. It is called the Goldsmith Beetle. It feeds upon the tender leaves of trees, and flies about only at night, and in the morning and evening twilight. In the daytime it hides on the under side of the leaves, and sometimes draws two or three leaves together, and holds them with its claws.

The Phaneus.

Some kinds of beetles have feelers ending in a knob, which is made up of several pieces; and they have toothed legs, and a plate which covers the face like the leather front of a boy's cap. These beetles are called Scarabæians, and they are very common. Every warm night in spring they come out of the ground — where they live in the grub state — and fly about. One kind is called the Dor-Bug, and when our windows are open in the spring and summer evenings it comes in, and with a buzzing sound flies around the room a few times, but, soon striking the walls, it falls upon the floor, where we can easily catch it and examine it. Some of the Scarabæians have very brilliant colors, and some have a horn on the head, as you see it in the picture of the Phaneus.

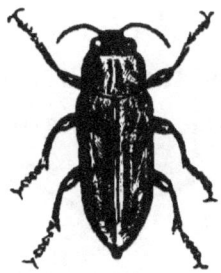

The Buprestis.

Some kinds of beetles like to stay, in the daytime, on the bark of the trees, and on the fences, where they can feel the warm sunshine. The Buprestis is a beetle of this kind. It is about an inch long and of a bronze color. It moves about slowly on the trees; and if you try to take it in your hand, it folds up its legs, and drops upon the ground and pretends to be dead. In the grub state it lives in the trunks of trees, where it bores holes in different directions, eating the wood, and doing great harm to the trees.

I think almost every child has seen the Spring-

Beetles, or Snap Beetles, which are so common in summer; they are often found in the house, on the window-sill or doorstep, and if you place one of these beetles on its back, it at once, with a snap and a jerk, throws itself upward, and this it keeps doing until it comes down right side up. The Spring-Beetles that we usually see are only about half an inch in length, but here is the

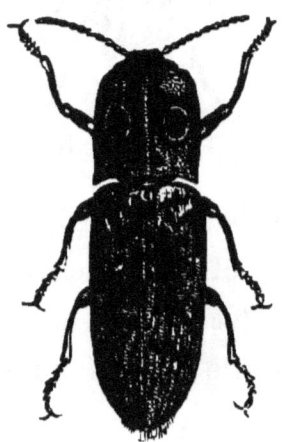

The Eyed Spring-Beetle.

picture of a very large one; it has on the upper part of its body two large oval spots which look like eyes, and from these it is named the Eyed Spring-Beetle. It is found upon trees, fences, and the sides of buildings.

The pretty "Fire-Flies" that you see at night upon the ground, shining like specks of flame, or flying about, sometimes so high in the air that they look like little twinkling stars, are small beetles which have the power of giving out a brilliant light. The Fire-Flies of Brazil, and other warm countries, are so large, and their light is so bright, that the people can see to work and to read by it. The Indians sometimes fasten these beetles to their moccasons, in order to light their path through the dark forests.

On the next page you may see pictures of five little beetles which are called Curculios, or Weevils. If you disturb these little insects, they fold up their legs and pretend to be dead; and if they are upon a tree or plant, they fall to the ground, and do not move till all is quiet again. The straight line near each beetle shows you its real length, for they are all drawn large so as to show their form. The Plum Weevil lays its eggs in plums, peaches, apples, cherries, and other fruits. The Rice Weevil feeds upon rice, and also upon wheat and Indian corn. The Pea Weevil lays its eggs in the tiny pods of the pea, and the little grubs live in the peas all winter and come out perfect beetles the next spring. The beautiful Golden Robins, or Baltimore Orioles, like to eat these little grubs, and so they come to the pea-vines and split open the pods and eat the peas in order to get the

The Plum Weevil, or Curculio.

The Rice Weevil.

The Pea Weevil.

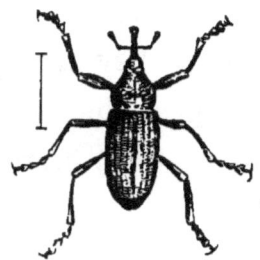

The White-Pine Weevil.

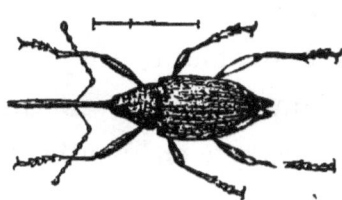

The Long-snouted Nut Weevil.

grubs, and perhaps they also like the tender peas. The White-Pine Weevil lays its eggs on the pine-trees, and almost always on the central and leading shoot; the grubs bore into the shoot, and gnaw in different directions, and thus they prevent the tree from growing into a tall, straight, and beautiful pine. Other kinds of weevils lay their eggs in nuts and acorns when they are small and soft, and the grub feeds upon the tender kernel; these are called Nut-Weevils.

Some kinds of beetles have such long curved feelers that they have been named the Long-horned Beetles. One of these, called the Painted Clytus, you will see late in the summer and in the early autumn, running up and down the trunks of the locust-trees; they are trying to find little crevices in the bark in which they may lay their eggs. These beetles like to eat the pollen or yellow dust of flowers, and you may often find them feeding upon the bright blossoms of the golden-rod. They are very beautiful little creatures; the body is velvet-black striped with yellow, and they have dark-brown feelers and reddish legs. The Beautiful Clytus is larger, and is seen in July.

One of the Long-horned Beetles is called the Apple-tree Borer, because when it is a grub it lives for two or three years in the trunk of the apple-tree, and, with its sharp jaws, gnaws long winding passages. It is also found in the trunks of thorn-trees and in quince-trees. The beetle is brown, with white stripes. It flies about only at night;

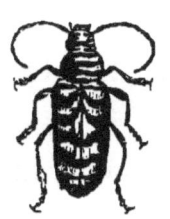

The Painted Clytus.

The Apple-tree Borer, — the perfect insect and grub.

in the daytime it hides among the leaves of the trees and plants upon which it feeds.

This large beetle is called the Broad-necked Pri-

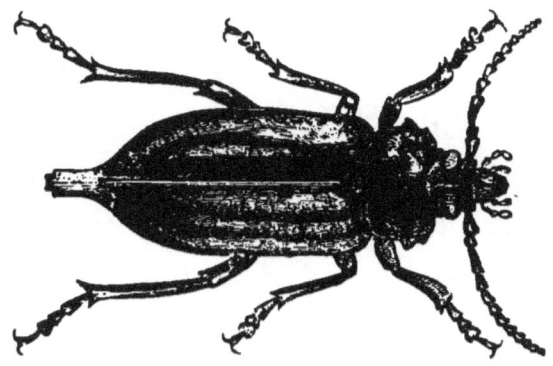

The Broad-necked Prionus.

onus. It gets the name of Prionus from a word which means a saw, because the feelers seem to be toothed like a saw, and sometimes the upper jaws are very long and toothed. The grub of this beetle lives in the trunks of the balm-of-gilead and poplar trees.

Here are pictures of three small but very pretty beetles. The Chrysomelan has a dark green head and body; its upper wings are silvery-white and green, and its thin under wings are rose-red. It lives upon the elm and linden trees, and feeds upon

The Chrysomelan.   The Cucumber Beetle.   The Lady-Bird.

their leaves. You may find the little Cucumber Beetle almost any day in summer on the cucumber, squash, and melon vines, for it is very fond of the tender leaves of these vines, and also of the pollen of the flowers. It often gets into the blossom as soon as it opens, and sometimes it is caught by the twisting and closing of the top of the flower, and, in order to get out, it is obliged to gnaw a hole through the side of its prison. You have often seen the pretty spotted Lady-Birds, for we find them upon many of our plants; but they do not feed upon the leaves, they eat the plant-lice, — little insects which often do our plants much harm.

THE CICADAS, &c., or HEMIPTERS.

In the warm days of summer, in July and August, you may hear the Cicadas singing among the branches of the elm-trees in the park or by the roadsides. You will look up into the trees

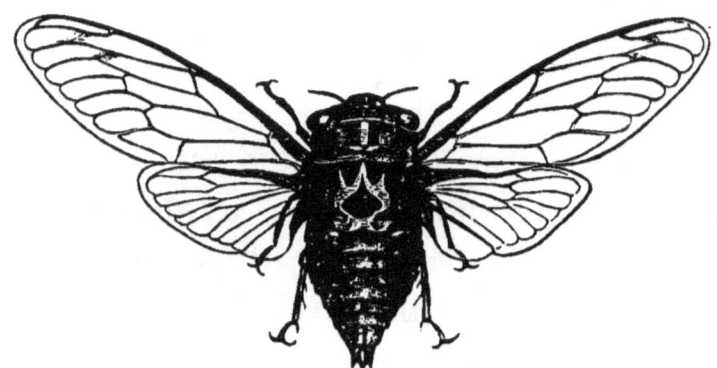

The Dog-day Cicada, or Harvest-Fly.

very eagerly to see one, but they keep so close to the limbs and leaves, and they are up so high, that you will have to look a long time, and perhaps many times, before you will get a glimpse of one. But I will show you its picture now, and tell you what its colors are, and then you will know the real one if you see it upon a tree, whether you hear it singing or not. The upper part of the body of the Cicada is black, marked with green lines; the under part is covered with a white substance which looks like flour; and its wings are large, thin, and very beautiful. The sound of its singing is clear and shrill, and so loud that sometimes it can be heard at the distance of a mile. But perhaps we ought not to call it singing, for it is not made by the mouth or throat, but by two little instruments, one on each side of the body, which are formed like little kettle-shaped drums. The people who lived long ago in Greece loved so much to hear the music of these little insects, that they often kept them in cages, and they called them the " Sweet Prophets of the Summer."

The Cicada lays its eggs in holes which it makes in the branches of trees, and the young ones, almost as soon as they are hatched, crawl to the side of the limb, let go their hold, and fall to the ground.

They then dig into the soil, and make their way to the roots of the tree, which they pierce with their sharp beak, and then feed upon the juices. When it is near the time for them to change into the winged form, they come towards the top of the ground, and there they live for several days, in the little burrows which they make in digging their way out. If the weather is warm and pleasant, they come to the top of the hole or burrow, and peep out, as if to see what is going on, but go down into the ground again if the weather grows cold or wet. At last, in the night, they come out of the ground and crawl up the trunk of a tree, or upon the fence, and cling firmly with the little claws of their feet. The skin is now dry, and after a while it splits on the back; the Cicada pushes out its head, draws out its body, leaving its empty skin still fastened to the tree, and looking a little way off very much like a large beetle. The Cicadæ are often called Harvest-Flies, and the one whose picture I have shown you is called the Dog-day Harvest-Fly, because it is often heard for the first time in the summer on the twenty-fifth day of July, the beginning of the Dog-days.

Here is a picture of a Cicada, which is said to be seen in the same region or place only once in

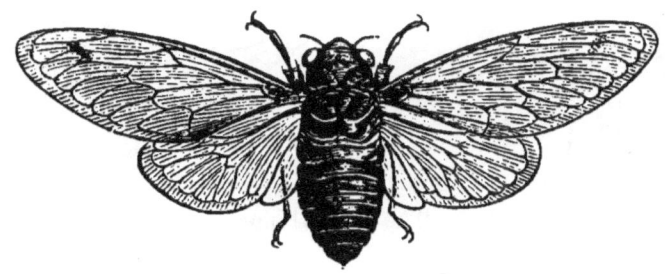

The Seventeen-year Cicada.

seventeen years, and so it is often called the Seventeen-year Locust. As it is not at all like a locust, but is a real Cicada, we will call it by its true name, which is Seventeen-year Cicada. The large veins and the borders of its wings and its eyes are red.

You will often see on trees, bushes, and on flowers, a curious-shaped little green creature, which, when you try to pick it up, will hop quickly away. It is called a Tree-Hopper, and it feeds upon the juices of plants. On the next page there are two pictures of it: one is drawn of the real size of the insect, and as it appears when you look upon its back, and the other is made large, and as it appears when you look at its side. In the early part of autumn you will see many of these little Tree-Hoppers upon the branches of

 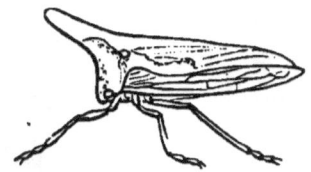

The Tree-Hopper.

the locust-trees, but as they always sit along the limb, and not across it, and as they have such a curious form, and are so quiet unless you put your fingers towards them, you might at first sight think they were only the little thorns of the tree.

Very often in the summer the edges of the leaves on the cherry and peach trees begin to curl, and at last the leaves on many of the branches, and perhaps on all of them, are so curled that the beauty of the tree is taken away. If you look at the leaves you will find on the under side a great number of little animals called Aphides, or Plant-Lice. They live upon all kinds of plants, and sometimes in such large numbers as to wholly cover the leaves. They have a very sharp beak with which they pierce the leaves, stems, and roots of plants so as to feed upon the sap. On the hind body there are two little tubes from which they give out small drops of a fluid which is as sweet as honey. Ants are very fond of this sweet fluid, and they crawl up the stems of plants and the trunks of trees in order to feed upon it. This is the reason that ants are so numerous upon the cherry-trees. Here is a picture of one of these little creatures. Its color is green; and it is very small, as you see by the straight mark in the corner, which shows you its real length.

The Aphis or Plant-Louse.

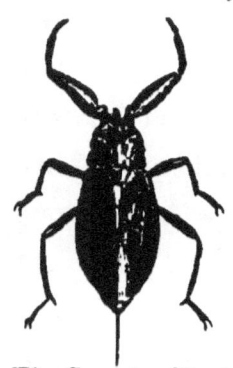

The Scorpion-Bug.

The Scorpion-Bug lives in ponds, slow-moving streams, and pools, and feeds upon little insects which it finds upon the plants that grow in the water. It seizes and holds them with its strong fore legs, which shut together like pincers. It has a very sharp sting.

As soon as the leaves of the squash-vines begin to grow, the Squash-Bugs come to them, and, in the night, lay their eggs in little clusters on the under side of the leaves; the eggs soon hatch into

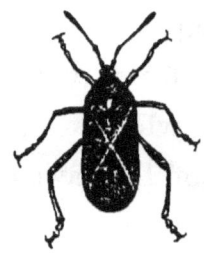

The Squash-Bug.

little bugs, which pierce the leaves and feed upon the sap. When the cold autumn weather comes they leave the vines, and crawl into little crevices in walls and fences, where they sleep all winter.

THE STRAIGHT-WINGED INSECTS, or ORTHOPTERS.

Here is a picture of the Earwig which lives under stones and under the bark of old trees, and

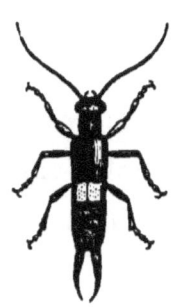

The Earwig.

which flies about only at night. Some people think that it will crawl into our ears when we are asleep, but we need not be afraid of it, for no one knows that it ever does so. At the hind part of the body it has a pair of sharp-pointed nippers, which it can open and shut like a pair of scissors. The Earwig eats fruits and the petals of flowers, and it is said to guard its eggs and young ones very carefully.

The Cockroaches live in kitchens, pantries, and closets, and they eat all kinds of food, and sometimes they eat clothing, carpets, and shoes, and

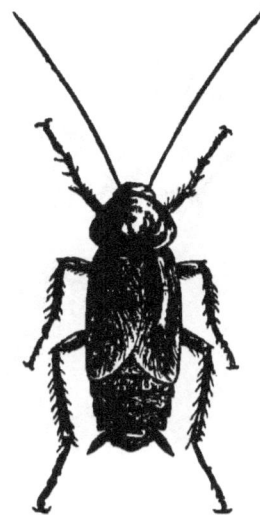

The Cockroach.

even the leather binding of books. They hide during the daytime, and at night, when all is dark and quiet, they come out of their holes and run over the floors, tables, and shelves.

On the next page there is a picture of a curious insect which has no wings, and which looks so much like a branching twig that it has been named the Walking-Stick. It crawls slowly, and often remains upon a branch or stem a long time without moving, and, as its color is a greenish-brown, it looks so much like a part of the branch

The Walking-Stick.

upon which it is, that you will not see it unless you look very closely. But late in the autumn, when the leaves of the trees have fallen, you may, perhaps, find it upon the ground and upon ledges of rock.

The Mantis is another very curious insect which lives upon trees and bushes. It feeds upon flies,

The American Mantis.

caterpillars, and other insects, and it has such a strange way of catching them that I am sure you will like to know about it. The Mantis crawls about slowly, or sits motionless, with its long fore legs stretched out and held up like arms, and, when any insect comes near, creeps towards it, then darts upon it with a spring, just as a cat darts upon a bird or mouse, seizes it, and kills it by squeezing it with its spiny fore legs, and then eats it. From its habit of holding up its fore legs, it has been named the Praying Mantis. Some of these insects have wings which look like green leaves, and others have wings that look like dry and slightly withered leaves.

The Crickets are little insects which you may see every day in summer, in the fields, in paths, and by the roadside; and you may hear their music, too, every summer night, and all the night long if you are awake. They are calling their mates, and they make the sounds which you hear by lifting the wing-covers, and rubbing them together. Many of these crickets are black, and are called the Field-Crickets. They eat the grass and tender plants, and often fruits and roots, and sometimes they kill and eat other insects. They lay their eggs in holes in the ground. When the cold weather comes, most of them die, but a few hide under stones and in holes, and so live through the winter. They are quarrelsome little creatures, and often fight fiercely with each other.

The House-Cricket lives in the cracks of floors and walls, and about the hearths and chimney-places, and its cheerful music is very pleasant to hear.

I must tell you that each kind of cricket and each kind of grasshopper has its own notes; no two kinds make the same noise or music.

On the next page there is a picture of a beautiful cricket which lives upon the stems and branches of shrubs and trees, and hides during the daytime among the leaves and flowers. It is called the Tree-Cricket, and sometimes the White Climbing-Cricket, for its color is white as ivory. The music of this little insect is loud and shrill, and it is heard from twilight until the dawn of day.

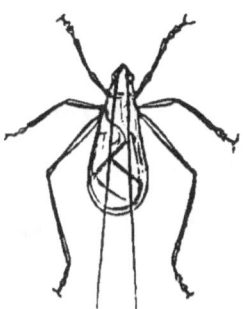

The White Climbing-Cricket.

But perhaps the most curious of all is the Mole-Cricket. Like the mole it lives in the ground in little burrows which it digs with its broad stout fore feet. It eats the roots of the grass,

The Mole-Cricket.

and in gardens it often does great harm by eating the roots of the vegetables and of the flowers.

The Katy-did looks like a large grasshopper.

It lives upon trees, and in the daytime is quiet and conceals itself among the leaves, or keeps close to the trunk or branch, but at night, and sometimes in cloudy days, just before night, it

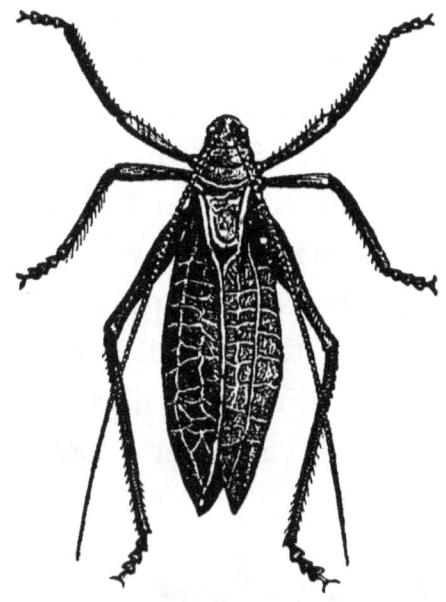

The Katy-did.

begins to sing, or to make the sounds which we call singing. These sounds seem to be like the words "Katy-did," and so the little insect is named the Katy-did. You will like to know how this music is made. In the upper part of each wing-cover, near where it is joined to the body, and where one wing-cover laps over the other, there is a little membrane, which looks somewhat like thin glass; this membrane is set in a sort of frame, and when the Katy-did opens and shuts its wing-covers, these frames are rubbed against each other, and thus the sounds are produced.

The color of the Katy-did is green, so it is not easy to see it among the leaves; but if you should see one, and put out your hand to take it, the little creature would quickly drop to some lower branch or twig, and then if, after another long search, you should find it, and try once more to put your hand over it, it would drop again. I saw a little Katy-did do this several times, until at last he dropped upon the ground; by quickly placing a hat over him, he was secured, and a pretty creature he was, with very long delicate feelers, and beautiful leaf-like wings.

You have often seen grasshoppers and locusts, for they live in every garden, and in the grass which grows by the roadside, as well as in the meadows and fields. They are so much alike that I must tell you how you may know one from the other. Grasshoppers have long and very slender feelers; Locusts have short and stout ones.

The eggs of these insects are laid in the ground, and the young ones hatch in the spring. At first

The Red-legged Locust or Grasshopper.

they have no wings, but they hop about without them, eat grass, grow very fast, and soon shed their skin. After a while the wings begin to grow on the top of the back; the little insect continues to eat and grow, and from time to time to shed its skin, until at last it comes out a perfect grasshopper, or locust, with thin, delicate, and often beautifully colored wings.

In the countries of the East, in Asia and Africa, locusts are sometimes seen in such immense swarms that they darken the sky like a cloud, and the noise that they make in flying is like the rushing of a whirlwind. In the Bible this noise is spoken of as being "like the noise of chariots on the tops of mountains." Wherever they alight, they eat up every green thing, so that famine and death follow in their track. Travellers have sometimes seen the locusts piled upon the ground to the depth of two feet, as far as the eye could reach! The ground over which they have passed looks as though it had been scorched by fire, and it is from this that they get the name of Locust, which is from a word that means a burnt place. The Emperor Alexander once sent out an army of thirty thousand soldiers to overpower an army of locusts. The soldiers formed a line, and advanced with shovels and collected the insects in sacks and burned them.

Some parts of our own country have at different times been overrun by locusts; and in one instance, in Kansas, a beautiful field of corn was attacked in the night by these insects, and the next morning not a blade was to be seen; every part had been eaten in one night!

THE NERVE-WINGED INSECTS, OR NEUROPTERS.

HERE is a picture of the May-Fly, a pretty little insect which lives only a few hours, or at the most only a day, after it gets its wings; and so it is

The May-Fly.

often called the Day-Fly. But in its larva form, that is, before it has wings, it lives for two or three years, and all of this time in the water, under stones, or in holes which it digs in the banks of ponds and streams. These holes or burrows are made below the surface of the water, in the soft soil, or, if made in coarse soil, they are lined with fine earth, and they have two openings, so that the little creature can go in, and come out again, without being obliged to back out, or to turn around in its little dwelling. When ready to change into the winged form, it swims to the top of the water, and bursts out of its pupa skin so quickly that it seems almost to fly out of the water. If you should see it at this time, you would believe it to be a perfect May-Fly, but it is really still covered with a very thin and delicate skin, so it flies to the shore and alights upon a plant or tree, and casts off this skin, and after this the wings are much brighter and the tails are longer. The May-Fly lays its eggs in the water, in little balls or clusters, each cluster containing several hundred eggs. These clusters, being heavier than the water, sink to the bottom of the river, or pond, and the eggs soon separate, and when the young ones hatch, they make the little homes that I have told you about.

May-Flies are sometimes seen in such immense

swarms that they darken the sky, the air being filled with them as you see it in winter filled with snow-flakes; and at such times they fall dead upon the ground in such numbers that the people collect their dead bodies in heaps to enrich the land.

The Stone-Fly, half-natural size.

The Stone-Fly also lives in the water in its young state, but after it gets its wings it lives much longer than the May-Fly. It lays its eggs on the rushes by the river-side.

Every pleasant day in summer you may see the Dragon-Fly skimming over the pools, ponds, and fields, its beautiful gauze-like wings glistening like gold in the sunshine. It is catching and eating mosquitoes and flies, and other insects upon which it feeds. Sometimes it flies into our rooms, and some little girls and boys are afraid of it, thinking it may sting them, but you need not be afraid of it, for it has no sting. This insect is often called a Darning-Needle, and you may

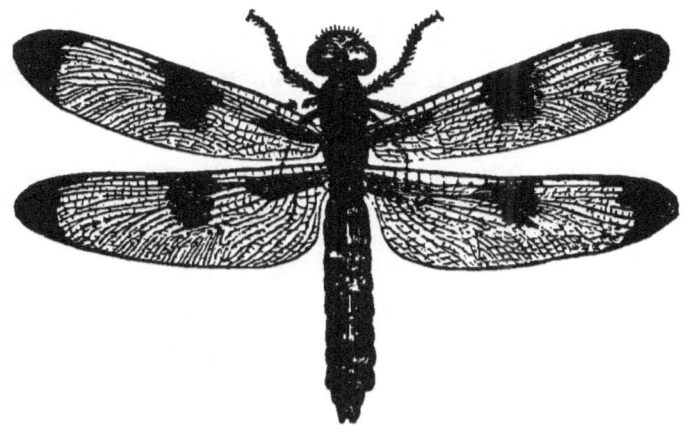

The Dragon-Fly.

have been told that it can sew your skin, but this is not true; it cannot harm you in any way. There are many kinds of Dragon-Flies, and their colors are often very beautiful. When young, they all live in pools, ponds, and ditches, and have long sprawling legs, and crawl about upon the mud at the bottom, and among the water-plants. They are very hungry creatures, and eat other water insects, tadpoles, and little fishes. When the time comes for them to leave the water, they crawl up the stems of plants, the skin splits open on the back, and the perfect Dragon-Fly comes forth, and, after drying itself in the sunshine, darts swiftly away.

The Horned Corydalis looks like a large Dragon-Fly with long horns. It also lives in the water

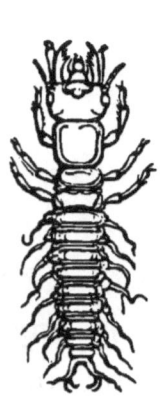

The Larva.

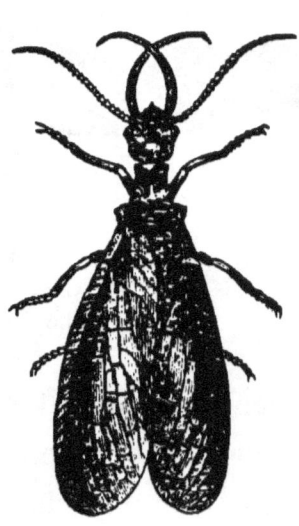

The Horned Corydalis.

in its young state. Here is a picture which shows you how it looks when it is living in the water, and

THE ANT-LION.

another which shows you how it looks when in the winged form.

The Ant-Lion has such thin delicate wings that it is often called the Lace-Wing. It is called the Ant-Lion, because in its young state it feeds upon ants and other insects; and it has a very odd way of catching the little creatures which it eats. It does not run after them, because it is so formed that it can move about only very slowly; so in order to get its prey it digs a pit in the sand,

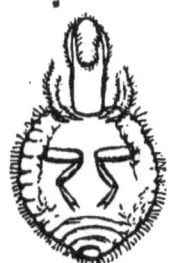 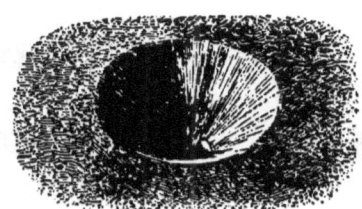

The Young Ant-Lion and its Pit or Trap.

as you see it in this picture, and then hides itself at the bottom of it, leaving only its jaws exposed. When an ant or any other small insect comes near the edge of the pit, the loose earth gives way under its feet, and it falls into the pit; the young Ant-Lion at once seizes it and eats it, and then hides again and waits for another insect to fall in. But perhaps I ought to tell you that the Ant-Lion does not eat the whole of these little insects; it only sucks their juices, and then casts the dry skin out of its pitfall. When the young Ant-Lion is ready to go into the pupa

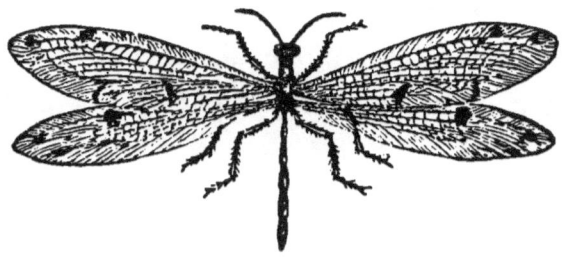

The Ant-Lion.

form, which is like the chrysalis form of the butterfly, it buries itself in the sand, and makes a little case out of the grains of sand, glueing them together by means of a sticky fluid which comes from its own body; and the inside is lined with fine and beautiful silken threads. It is said to stay in this little case for about two months, and then comes forth with its lace-like wings, and looks as you see it in the picture. It lays its eggs in the sand.

THE CADDICE-FLY.

On the bottom of nearly every pool and brook you may find, at almost any time when you will take the trouble to look for them, little cases made of bits of broken shells, or of coarse sand, or of grass, twigs, or pieces of bark; you will see these little cases moving about, and if you look closely at one of them you will see, at one end, a little head and six legs. The little animals which make these cases and live in them are young Caddice-

The Caddice-Fly.

Flies. The case is open at both ends, and it is softly lined with silk, and the pieces of which it is made are held together by threads of silk. The little insect within is quite secure from harm, and crawls slowly about and feeds mainly upon the plants that grow in the water. When it has grown to its full size, it creeps up the stem of some plant, until the opening of its case is just even with the top of the water, and then it spins a web of silk across the case and goes into the pupa form, and by and by comes out with wings, and looks as you see it in the picture.

THE SPIDERS.

I will now tell you about the Spiders. You do not like to see them so well as you like to

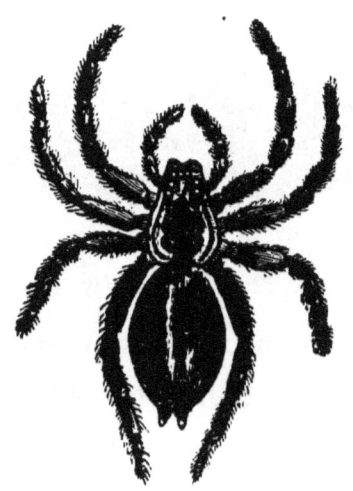

The Spider.

see the pretty bees, butterflies, and beetles; but they are very curious creatures, and some of them have very beautiful colors. All of the insects whose pictures I have shown you, and which I have told you about, have the body divided into three parts, — a head, a middle part, and a hind body; and they have six legs, and either two or four wings. But the Spiders have the body divided into only two parts, — a head and the hind body; and they have eight legs, and two large feelers that look like legs, and none of them have wings. There are many kinds of spiders, and all of them spin some sort of a web. You have often seen spider-webs in the barn, and shed, and on the bushes, and on the ground, and in the house. These webs are snares or traps to catch flies, and other insects which the spiders like to eat, and which it would be very difficult for them to get, because they have no wings, were it not for the webs that they spin. Sometimes the webs of the large spiders, in warm countries, are so strong that little birds, which happen to fly against them, get entangled in the meshes and cannot get away.

The House Spider spins a net-like web in the corners of the rooms. A naturalist named Goldsmith has told of one which lived for three years in a corner of his room, and grew so tame that it would come and take a fly from his hand. A story is told of a House-Spider which lived in a room where there was a piano, and whenever any one played upon the piano he would come out of his retreat, and let himself down by spinning a silken thread, and hang over the piano until the music ceased, when he would go back again.

The Geometer Spider makes a web among the bushes in the garden, or in an open window in the barn or shed. It is made in the most beautiful manner, the lines running from the centre, like the spokes in a wagon-wheel, and these are joined by a line which at first sight seems to be arranged in circles, but which is really only one line which the spider starts at the centre and carries round and round to the outside.

The Mason or Trap-Door Spider builds its nest in the ground. It first digs a deep pit, sometimes one or two feet long, which it lines all around with silk, making a warm and comfortable home, and then it begins to build the door, — the most curious part of this little dwelling. The spider spins a little web which is just as large as the mouth of the hole, but joined to it only at one point on the upper side; then it covers this web with soil, and then spins another layer of silk, and covers this with soil; and it keeps doing this until the door is made thick and strong enough. The outside layer is of soil, so the little home of the spider is not easy to find. The point where the door is joined to the ground serves as a hinge and the door opens outward by the pressure of the spider against it, and shuts by its own weight. If any one tries to open this door, the spider runs to it, and fixes some of its little claws in the silk which lines it, and others in the silk which lines its home, and pulls with all its might to keep the door closed.

Some kinds of spiders have a silken den near their web, or in one part of it, in which they stay most of the time. They spin lines from this den to different parts of the web, and when a fly or any other little insect gets entangled in the web, they know it by the quivering of these lines, and dart out and run to the little creature and bite it, poisoning it so that it soon dies. If the insect be very large and strong, the spider waits till the insect gets more entangled, and at last, tired out by its efforts to get away; then it binds it with its siken threads, and begins to eat it up. The bite of a common spider is so poisonous that it kills a fly; the bite of some kinds which live in South America kills little birds; and men are sometimes killed by a spider's bite. Spiders lay eggs and enclose them in silken sacs. Some kinds carry this egg-sac about with them; others spin it in a safe place, and stay near to watch it till the young are hatched, and to tear it open so that the young may crawl out. Perhaps you have seen some of the little egg-sacs; they are often made of the whitest, finest, and most beautiful silk, and some of them are very curious in their

A Spider's Nest.

form. Here is the picture of one which was found upon a grape-vine. It looks like a vase, and it was bound to the vine by many fine silken threads, as you can see by looking at the picture.

Spiders do not spin their silk in the same way that caterpillars do; but they have in the hind part of the body a very curious organ, called the spinneret, by which the delicate threads of the spider-web are spun. This organ is made of four or six knobs, and in each knob there are a thousand holes, and through these holes the minute silken threads pass out, more than four thousand at a time; and at a little distance from the knobs all these minute threads unite into one, forming the thread which you have often seen. The silk comes from a sticky fluid contained in bags in the hind body; and when the threads first come out of the knobs they are soft, but they harden into silk as soon as the air touches them.

The length of the line which a spider spins is sometimes very great. Dr. Wilder, of Boston, wound in a few hours, from a curious spider which he found in South Carolina, a line of the most beautiful silk, nearly two miles long!

The spider-web has other uses besides that of catching flies and other insects for its owner.

The men and the women who study the stars, and look through the telescope every clear night, have spiders' lines stretched across each other in the telescope, so as to guide their eyes, in a way which you can understand when you are a little older. Silk garments have been made from the spider's silk; and Dr. Wilder believes that the curious spider which he found in South Carolina will some time be kept and tended in large numbers, and that we shall get silk for ribbons and for dresses from it, as we now do from the silkworm which I have told you about on another page.

Scorpions are spider-like animals which have a long body ending in a curved sharp sting. It is very dangerous to handle, or even to touch them, for their sting is very poisonous, often causing death. They live only in warm countries. The one whose picture is on the next page lives in Texas. Scorpions lurk under stones, and under rubbish, and in caves, or other damp and dark places, and sometimes they are found in houses. They run very fast, bending the long hind body in every direction, and striking this way and that, so as to wound whatever touches them. With their sting they kill locusts, beetles, and other insects, which they catch by means of their pincers. The Scorpion carries her young ones upon her back during

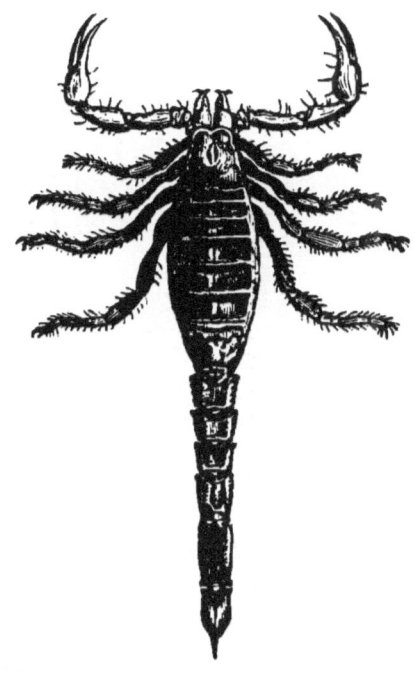

The Scorpion.

the first few days of their life, and watches over them and cares for them until they are able to take care of themselves. Scorpions will not bear imprisonment; if one is shut up in a box, or a glass vessel, as soon as it finds that it cannot get away, it stings itself to death.

THE CENTIPEDES.

Here is a picture of a small animal which you will often find under rubbish, and under the stones

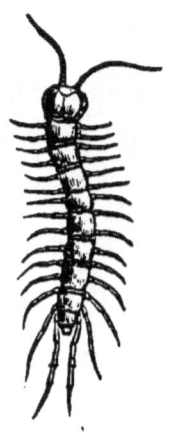

The Lithobius.

in the garden. It is called a Centipede, a word which means hundred feet. It is sometimes called an earwig, but that is not its right name. A true earwig has large and very beautiful wings; this little creature has no wings, but it has so many pairs of feet that it can run very fast. In hot countries centipedes grow to be very large, and their bite is more dangerous than the sting of the scorpion. They creep into houses and hide under furniture, and in drawers and closets, and sometimes they are found even in beds. They feed upon insects and worms.

Here is a picture of a little animal which you may sometimes see crawling slowly along upon

The Galley-Worm.

the ground, but which you find oftener under stones and moss, and under the bark and in the wood of old decaying trees. This one is called a Millepede, a word which means thousand feet. It may also be called the Galley-Worm. If you touch one of these little animals, it quickly coils itself so that it looks like a little snail-shell. It feeds upon decaying wood, roots, and leaves, and it lays its eggs in the ground, or in the dust of old dead wood. When the young are first hatched they have no legs, but in a few days they throw off their first skin, and then appear with three pairs of legs. In a few days more they change their skin again, and then they have seven pairs of legs; and this they keep on doing until they get their full number of legs.

THE CRABS, LOBSTERS, AND SHRIMPS.

CRABS are queer-looking animals which you find among the rocks and under the sea-weeds, when you go to the sea-shore in the summer. They are covered by a shell, have ten legs, and, what

A Crab.

is very curious, they can walk backward and sidewise as well as forward. Two of their feet end in claws, which they use to pick up their food, and to crush it, and they bite so severely with these claws, that if one should get hold of your hand you could not easily get it away.

There are a great many kinds of these animals. Some of them are no larger than a penny; others are as large as your hand; others are as large as a saucer; and others are larger than the plate from which you eat your dinner. Some kinds live on the sands and among the rocks far down in the sea; others live in the shallow waters near the shore; others live on the rocky and sandy beaches, where the waves may dash over them; others live on the shore in burrows; and others live all the time upon the land, far from the sea, upon hills and mountains, going to the sea only to lay their eggs. Those that live on the land are the Land Crabs, and they are found only in warm countries. They live in holes which they dig in the ground, and often in the hollow stumps of trees, and in the clefts of the rocks. In the spring they come out of their holes, and get together in large troops, and march in a straight line for the sea. They travel mostly in the night, and it is said that nothing but large rivers can turn them from their path, and that they march over houses, and scale rocks, and often injure and destroy whole plantations as they pass along.

Many people like crabs for food. The one shown in the picture — the Soft-shelled Crab — is caught in great numbers on our coast, and sold in the markets of New York, and Philadelphia, and other

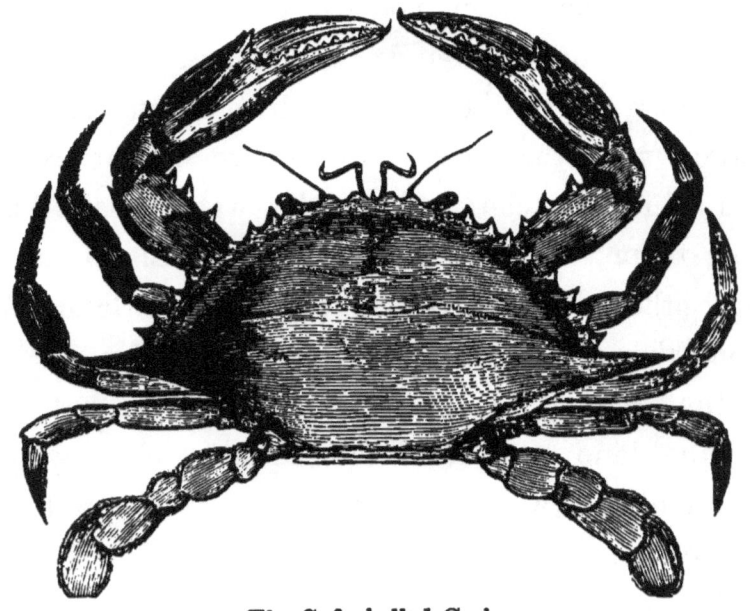

The Soft-shelled Crab.

cities. This kind, as well as others, can live for several days out of water, if kept in a moist place. The one whose picture you see here was carried from New York to Boston, in a box containing damp grass, and the little fellow was alive and well at the end of his journey.

THE CRABS.

The Fiddler Crab is very small, and it gets its name from the form of one of its claws, which is much larger than the other, and shaped somewhat like the bow of a fiddle. These crabs live in burrows on the sea-shore, and they close the

The Fiddler Crab.

opening to their burrow by means of their large claw. They have a habit of flourishing this claw, as if they were beckoning to some one far off, and so they are sometimes called the Calling Crabs. They stay in their burrows all winter.

But perhaps the most curious of all the crabs is the one which is called the Hermit Crab. It gets this name from its habit of living by itself, and the singular manner in which it obtains a home. You will like to know why and how it does this. Its long hind body, instead of being covered by a hard shell, is soft like leather, and so it would easily be injured if the little animal did not find some protection or shelter for it. But this is just what he does; he crawls about on the shore, where the shells are thrown by the waves, or left by the tide, seeking for an empty shell which may serve him as a dwelling-place; and when he finds one of the right size, he inserts his tail, and retreats into the shell, and thus secures a safe abode. At the end of the tail there is a little organ, a sort of sucker, by which the crab is able to attach itself firmly to the shell, which it now carries about wherever it goes. When walking or eating, the head and legs extend beyond the shell, but when alarmed the crab withdraws into the shell, and closes the opening with its large claw; for one of its claws is much larger than the other. When the Hermit Crab has grown somewhat larger, it is obliged to change its abode, so it crawls along the beach searching for a larger shell, and it is very amusing to watch him in his search. He tries first one shell and then another, until at last he finds one which suits him. Another name for this animal is Soldier Crab; for sometimes, when it cannot find an empty dead shell which suits it for a home, it will attack a living one, and fight until it gets possession of it.

The Lobsters are curious animals which live in the sea. They have a large and lòng hind

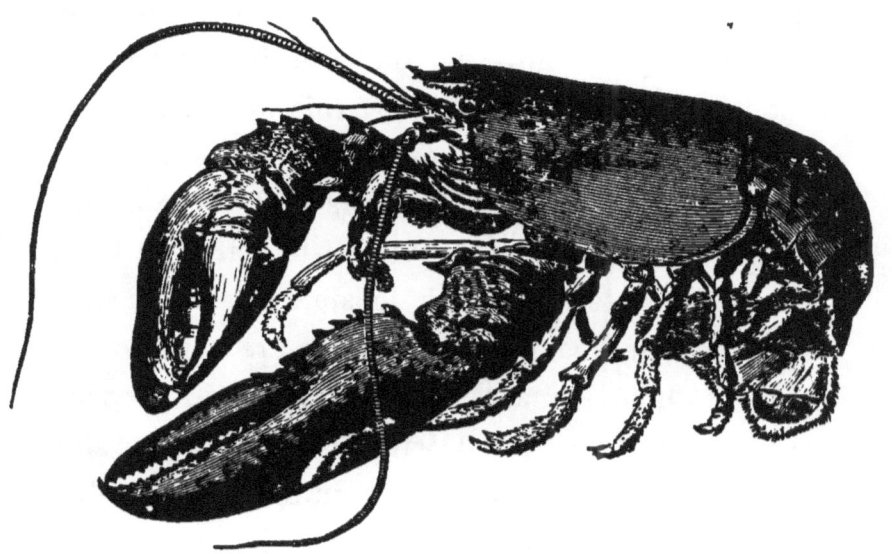

The Lobster.

body, which is almost always turned forward, as you see it in the picture. Two of their legs are very large, and end in strong claws or pincers, and one of these claws has blunt rounded teeth suited for crushing shells, and the other has very sharp teeth suited for biting. These claws are so powerful that a lobster can easily bite off a man's finger with them; and if one of them were to get hold of your hand, you could not get it away, without breaking off the lobster's claw. The fishermen, or men who catch lobsters, know well their biting habits, and when they catch a lobster they put a wooden plug into the joints of its pincers, so that it cannot open them. If this were not done, the lobsters might not only bite the fishermen, but they would bite off the legs and claws of one another when confined in the lobster-car, — a large box in the water in which lobsters are kept alive after they are caught, until they are sent to the market. Lobsters are caught mainly in wooden traps, which are baited with fish. On one side is a door which opens easily into the trap, but which does not swing outward; so when the lobster is once in, he cannot get out again.

In crawling about over the rocks, and on the bottom of the sea, the lobster moves rather slowly, but sometimes, by a single stroke of its powerful tail, or hind body, it darts backward in the water many feet, with the swiftness of an arrow.

When a lobster, or a crab, or any other crustacean, as these animals are called, because of the crust or shell with which they are furnished, loses a leg, or a feeler, or any other organ, even an eye, another like it grows to supply its place. You may have seen in the market lobsters with one claw much smaller than the other; the small one is a newer or younger claw, and has grown in the place of one which has been lost. Lobsters have the power of throwing off their claws, and it is said that the firing of a gun over one which was freshly caught caused it, in its terror, to throw off both its claws.

But one of the most interesting and wonderful facts about lobsters, and other crustaceans is, that from time to time, until they get their full growth, they shed the shell in one piece, so that the cast-off shell looks exactly like the perfect animal; feelers, eyes, jaws, legs, and even every hair, are all just as they were when they covered the live lobster! The lobster comes out of his shell through a rent on the back, and at first he is very soft; he grows rapidly, and in a few days his skin is as hard as the shell which he cast off. It is in this way that the lobsters and other crustaceans grow; for while the shell remains, the animal can only grow just large enough to fill it. When a lobster is ready to shed its shell, there are two hard, stone-like bodies at the sides of the stomach; and it is supposed that these furnish a part of the solid matter for the new shell, for after the shedding they begin to grow smaller, and soon disappear entirely.

The little Craw-Fish, or Fresh-Water Lobster, lives in brooks, streams, and springs. One kind lives on the Western prairies and in the Southern States, in holes which it digs in the ground deep enough to find water. Those that live in our brooks hide in burrows and under stones on the banks, and come out to feed upon small fishes and little mollusks. The Craw-Fish is about three inches long.

Lobsters and Craw-Fishes, or Cray-Fishes, for they are called by both names, carry their eggs under the hind body or tail, and the young ones also nestle there for shelter and protection.

On the next page there is a picture of the Shrimp, whose home is in the sea. This little animal is only about two inches long; its body is half transparent, and of a green color, like the ocean, so that it is not easy to see it in the water. It is also said to burrow in the sand, leaving only its eyes exposed, and in this way it often watches

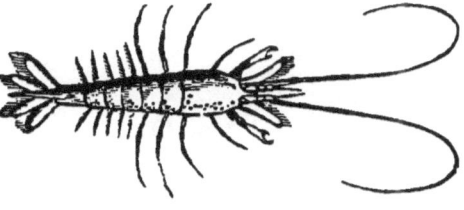

The Shrimp.

for its prey. There are many kinds of shrimps, some of them four or five inches in length, or more. Many fishes and water-birds feed upon shrimps, and large numbers of them are also caught in nets for food.

THE SAND-HOPPERS AND TRILOBITES.

If you have ever been upon the sea-beach in summer-time, you have seen the little animals called Sand-Hoppers. These little creatures burrow in the sand and seldom enter the water. They feed upon the small animals which are thrown upon the beach by the tide and the waves, and they like to eat the worms which live in the sand along

The Sand-Hopper.

the shore, and they often attack those that are ten or twenty times their own size.

A great many thousand years ago, when the ocean was much larger than it is now, and when it covered the place where we now live, and nearly all the places which you ever saw, very many kinds of animals lived in the waters unlike any that are living now. Many of these animals became buried in the sand and mud at the bottom of the sea, and when the sea bottoms were lifted up out of the water so as to become dry, the sand and mud were hardened into rocks, and when we break open these rocks we find some of the animals that lived and died so long ago. Some kinds of these animals are star-shaped; some kinds look like the shells which you find on the sea-shore now; and others look like worms; and others look like the picture which you see here; and some are fishes. The Trilobite is one of these

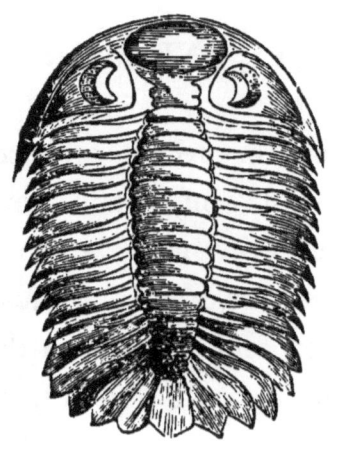

The Trilobite.

old animals, and it is found in the rocks in many places in this country and in other countries. It is named from its three lobes or divisions. Some of the Trilobites were no larger than a penny, others were almost twice as long as this book. They lived near or on the bottom of the old oceans, and they looked a little like the Horse-Shoe Crabs which are very common on the sea-coasts now. When you go to Trenton Falls in New York, you may get some one to break open the black limestone rocks which you will see there, and you will find a Trilobite in them.

THE BARNACLES AND HORSE-SHOE CRAB.

Among the many curious and beautiful objects which will interest you, when you visit the sea-shore in summer, are the little acorn-shaped shells which cover the rocks and stones in every spot where the waves and spray can dash over them. These are the Acorn-Barnacles, and here is a

The Acorn-Barnacle.

picture of one of them, as it looks when it is out of the water. But if you should take a stone, covered with these little shells, fresh from the sea, and put it in a basin of sea-water, and watch the shells closely, you would see them begin to open, and very soon beautiful feather-like feelers would be thrust out, and then withdrawn, then thrust out again, and again withdrawn; and the little creatures would keep doing this so regularly and so gracefully, that you would be quite delighted with watching them. You will like to know why they do this; they are trying to find something which they will like to eat, — very minute animals, and the little particles of food that may be floating about in the water. They have no eyes, and so cannot see to pick up anything, but these soft, delicate, feathery feelers are very sensitive, and when they touch a particle of food, or a little animal, it is quickly drawn to the mouth and eaten. And more than this, the opening and shutting of these little shells, and the waving and grasping of these tiny arms, cause little currents and whirlpools in the water, and these little currents and whirlpools bring many little floating particles of food within the reach of the Acorn-Barnacles, and thus they are able to get plenty to eat, although they cannot move about from place to place. But the strangest part of their history is yet to be told; for these little creatures have not always been fixed to the rocks and stones where we now see them, nor have they always been without eyes. When young they were of quite a different form, and they had large eyes, and several pairs of swimming legs, and they swam and leaped about in the water, until at last they shed their shell, and became fixed to a rock or a stone, or some other object in the water, and then their eyes began to disappear, their arms to grow, and they changed gradually into the little acorn-shaped animals that I have told you about.

Other kinds of barnacles grow in clusters, and are attached by stems to floating wood, to the

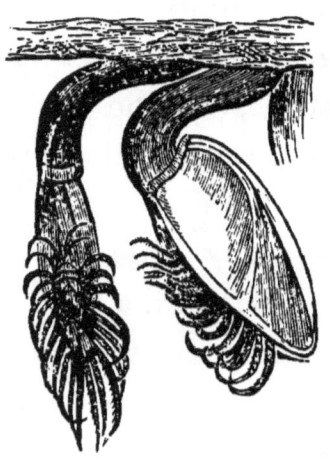

The Goose Barnacle.

bottom of ships, to the timbers of wharves, and also to shells, turtles, fishes, whales, and other sea animals. These stemmed barnacles, when young, also floated and swam about in the water, like the young Acorn-Barnacles. The resemblance of the beautiful feather-like arms of barnacles to the feathers of birds, caused the people who lived many years ago to believe that these animals were the young of the barnacle geese, and that at last they came forth from their shells as real birds!

You will scarcely believe that barnacles can have any power over, or in any way influence, the motion of a large ship; but, in long voyages, they sometimes so completely cover the bottom of a ship, that they greatly hinder its progress through the water.

On the next page is a picture of a queer-looking animal that is often seen upon the sea-shore. It is called the Horse-shoe Crab, because its broad, thin shell is shaped somewhat like the hoof of a horse. The body ends in a long hard spine, and the point of the spine is very sharp. The savages on the islands of the sea use these spines for spear-heads and arrow-points. The Horse-shoe Crab has several pairs of organs fitted for swimming about in the water, and several other pairs fitted for crawling on the shore; the crawling legs are situated around the mouth of this queer creature, and serve as its jaws also, and at the upper part they are furnished with teeth and spines for biting and

The Horse-shoe Crab.

crushing the food; so that the Horse-shoe Crab walks and eats with the same organs! This crab cannot bear the heat of the sun, and it is said that when left by the waves upon the shore, where it cannot easily crawl into the water, it will bury itself in the sand for a shelter.

THE WORMS.

The last story in this book is about the Worms. But perhaps you are thinking that they are ugly looking little things, and good for nothing except fish-baits, and that you do not care to read about them. If you have been thinking so, then I must tell you first that the worms are interesting and very useful animals, and some of them are as beautiful as the most beautiful flowers that grow in your little garden.

Some kinds of worms live in the ground; other kinds live in the mud at the bottom of ponds and rivers; but the greatest numbers live in the sea, and these are the most wonderful and the most beautiful of all.

The Earth-Worm.

Of those that live in the ground, the most common is the Earth-Worm, which every child has often seen, and which men and boys often use for bait when they fish for the beautiful speckled trout. The Earth-Worm, in some cases, is made up of more than a hundred rings, and it has neither eyes, nor feelers, nor feet, but it has, on each ring of its body, four pairs of bristles or spines, which stand backward, and these aid it in making its way through the ground, which it pierces in every direction. In this way the Earth-Worms work over the soil, and make it looser, lighter, and more fertile, and thus they are of great benefit to the farmer and gardener. The Earth-Worms are very useful in another way, for they are the food of many kinds of animals. The little moles that live in the ground eat them; the woodcock and many other kinds of birds feed upon them; the frogs and toads, and even the fishes, are glad to get Earth-Worms to eat.

The Leeches, or Bloodsuckers, are worms which live in ponds and streams, and also in the sea, and there are very many kinds of them. They are very hungry creatures, and they feed upon other animals. They attach themselves to frogs, fishes, snails, and worms, and suck out their blood and soft parts, and they sometimes devour one another. When the cold weather comes, they bury themselves in the mud at the bottom of the ponds and streams, and sleep all winter, and in the spring crawl out and swim about again.

The Hair-Worm, or Gordius, is another curious worm which lives in the water. It is about as large as a horsehair, and some people think that it is a hair from a horse's mane or tail, and that it has been changed to a worm by lying in the water! But I need not tell you that hairs never change into worms. When the Hair-Worm is young, it lives in the body of an insect, sometimes that of the water-beetle, and when grown, it leaves the body of the insect, and escapes into the water. It lays its eggs in long chains, in the water, or in some moist place; and when the young ones are hatched they eat their way into the body of some insect, and there they live until they get their growth and are ready to come forth into the water, where you see them.

But it is in the sea that we find those wonderfully beautiful worms, whose colors are as brilliant, and whose hues are as varied, as the many-tinted flowers of the garden. Unlike the worms that I have been telling you about, which have no breathing organs that we can see, these splendid creatures have breathing organs of the most elegant forms, and of the richest colors. But I must first tell you that while some of the sea-worms are free, and move about from place to place, burrowing in the sand at the bottom of the ocean, or swimming about in the water, other sea-worms cannot move about at all, for they live either in beautiful shelly tubes, that are formed around them as they grow, or in tubes which they build of sand, little stones, and shells, and other materials which they find in the sea, — the fragments of which these tubes are built being fastened together with a sticky substance which comes from the body of the worm.

The sea-worms that are free have their breathing organs, or gills, arranged along the sides of the body, in the form of delicate fringes, or in tufts which look like miniature trees; while those sea-worms that live in tubes have their breathing organs arranged around the head and neck in the form of collars, plumes, and crests.

Of those sea-worms that move about freely in

the water, one of the most beautiful is called the Sea-Mouse, because it is clothed with silky hairs. These hairs have the shining lustre of gold, silver, and other metals, and they reflect all the hues of the rainbow, — red, orange, yellow, green, blue, indigo, and violet; and the feathers upon the breast of a humming-bird, or the wing-covers of the most brilliant beetles, are not more splendid than the colors of this little worm of the sea.

Some of the tube-building worms make their little homes of sand; these live on the shores and beaches of the sea, where the tide can flow over and cover them; and when the water covers them they present a most beautiful appearance, for out of the opening of each little tube there comes a little head and neck; the neck is adorned with rings of golden hair, and around the head are feathery, plume-like tufts of beautiful colors, and the whole looks like a bed of bright flowers.

You may sometimes see upon the sea-shore, when the tide is out, beautiful tubes made of shining pearly bits of broken shells, and grains of sand, little pebbles of different colors, with here and there small whole shells. Each one of these little tubes has been the home of a sea-worm named the Terebella. These worms have around the head long delicate feelers, which stretch out far and wide, and adhere to the little specks of sand and bits of shell; these they bring together, piece by piece, and arrange them in the form of a circular wall, fastening them together with the gluey secretion which comes from their body. These sea-worms are often kept in Aquaria, and it is very interesting and pleasant to watch them while they are building their curious and pretty homes. Some kinds of Terebellæ live together in groups, and the clusters of tubes which they form are sometimes quite large.

The sea-worms called Serpulæ live in white shelly tubes which are formed around them as they grow. They are almost always found in clusters which are attached to the surface of a stone, or a shell, or to any object that has been a long time in the sea; sometimes they are attached along their whole length, at other times they are attached only for a part of their length. The tubes are often coiled and twisted, and it is from this coiling and twisting that they get the name of Serpulæ, a word which means to twist about like serpents. One end of the tube tapers to a point, and is closed; the other end is

The Serpula.

open, and from this the head, with its beautiful crest-like cluster of gills, comes forth. The colors of these clusters of gills are of the brightest scarlet and crimson, owing to the blood which is all the time flowing through them; and these little sea-worms, when expanded, are as beautiful as the most brilliant carnations when in full blossom.

The tube of the Serpula is often much longer

than the worm itself, and it serves as a safe retreat for the little creature; for when danger is near, the Serpula quickly draws in its head, and the opening to the tube is beautifully closed by a little organ called the "stopper." You can see this little organ in the picture of the Serpula; it is one of the harder portions of the worm, and it is often found in the shelly tube long after the soft parts of the animal have disappeared. Although the Serpula darts so quickly into his tube that you can scarcely follow his movements with the eye, he is very slow in coming out again, expanding his tufts or gills in the most cautious manner.

The sea-worms are beautiful objects for the Aquarium, and there we can study them and learn their structure and habits; and the more we watch them and study them, the more we shall see in them to excite our interest and our wonder; and thus we shall learn that the humblest creatures that God has made are full of beauty, and full of interest, and full of instruction.

THE END.

www.ingramcontent.com/pod-product-compliance
Lightning Source LLC
Chambersburg PA
CBHW030350170426
43202CB00010B/1321